ULTIMATE TRAINING FOR THE MARTIAL ARTS

Edited by
John R. Little and Curtis F. Wong

CB
CONTEMPORARY BOOKS

Library of Congress Cataloging-in-Publication Data

Ultimate training for the martial arts / edited by John R. Little and
Curtis F. Wong.
    p.   cm.
   ISBN 0-8092-2834-3 (acid-free paper)
   1. Martial arts—Training.   I. Little, John R.   II. Wong, Curtis.

GV1102.7.T7U48   2001
796.8—dc21   00-56991

Contemporary Books

A Division of The **McGraw-Hill** *Companies*

3 4 5 6 7 8 9 0 VLP VLP 0 5 4 3 2

ISBN 0-8092-2834-3

This book was set in Perpetua-OsFNTC
Printed and bound by Vicks Lithograph & Printing Corporation

Cover design by Todd Petersen
Cover and interior photographs courtesy of CFW Enterprises
Interior illustrations by Susan Spellman

McGraw-Hill books are available at special quantity discounts to use as premiums and
sales promotions, or for use in corporate training programs. For more information, please
write to the Director of Special Sales, Professional Publishing, McGraw-Hill, Two Penn
Plaza, New York, NY 10121-2298. Or contact your local bookstore.

This book is intended to provide general information and advice on exercise. It is not
intended to provide specific health advice or recommendations pertaining to any
individual's condition. If you are uneasy about following the exercise strategies explained
in this book; if you have a medical condition that prevents you from performing these
exercises; if you have high blood pressure, heart disease, or a chronic illness; if you are
pregnant or nursing an infant; or if you are taking other medications, you should consult
with your medical doctor. The authors and publisher are not responsible for any health
problems resulting from your following the exercises in this book.

This book is printed on acid-free paper.

Contents

PART 4: OTHER HEALTH AND TRAINING CONSIDERATIONS

PART 5: NUTRITION

Part 6: Technique Training for Striking, Kicking, and Grappling

Part 7: Weapons Training

Part 8: Injuries

Part 9: Sparring

PART 1

Power Training

Triple Your Punching Power Overnight

Royce Bunch

Today we are experiencing an upsurge in the health industry. Companies tapping into the cash flow are busy trying to build the ultimate piece of equipment that will give an individual the perfect workout. I have tried and own several pieces of equipment and have found only a few that really work.

Most pieces offer, at best, only minimal physical improvement, and can be expensive to own. Some people feel compelled to purchase every new piece of equipment made available, even if they have only rarely used the equipment they already have.

The martial arts industry is not immune to the side effects of the growth in the health industry. We strive to develop the newest, most innovative training methods to go along with the newest and most innovative training devices. I am not saying this is all bad.

The Ladder of Success

Dr. John Win Lok Ng, a well-known *kung-fu* grandmaster, once said, "Many people training today in martial arts are like the person who begins to climb a ladder, while setting fire to the bottom of this ladder. He sets the fire so there is no way but up, which then forces him to climb very fast. He reaches the platform or level above, only to find there is another level beyond the one reached. He now needs to pull up the ladder to climb higher, but to his dismay, finds his ladder burned and gone. He is now at a certain level yet cannot go higher, because he cannot go lower."

The ladder and its rungs represent the basics, which have been proven to work time and time again. These basics were born in a time when people faced the threat of death every day. There's nothing wrong with creating new methods, but often we discard old ideas for the sake of the latest invention, even without proof that the latest method has any merit.

There are many ways to develop a more powerful punch, and probably just as many new machines and concepts to supplement this process. Dr. Ng possessed almost superhuman power. He has been known to strike an individual from only a few inches with devastating results, hurling the poor soul backward by a seemingly invisible powerful force. People who witnessed his grasp of power were amazed. But his ability did not come easily; his training began early in his youth in China and continued into adulthood. His grandfather, Mak Jack Man, taught him the secrets for developing short power.

Long on Results

With short power, you can strike from a short distance with enough power to injure an opponent. Short power is practiced not only in Chinese styles, but also in many other styles. The ability, however, is seldom demonstrated and often hidden within the framework of the poison hand arts.

Today, as the veil of secrecy is slowly lifted, more of these special skills are being taught. The ability gained by practicing short power is well worth the effort required. The techniques explained here were taught to me by my *sifu* master Ricky Pickins, who learned the skill from Dr. Ng.

The technique of short power can be used with iron palm, vibration palm, phoenix fist, or any number of other systems. Even if you do not have training in any of the poison hand arts, you will find that you can double or even triple your punching power by constantly practicing this technique. Best of all, equipment needed for short power is very inexpensive.

For a technique to possess value, regardless of style, it must address a need. Short power gives a practitioner the ability to deliver short, explosive punches, allowing the user to conceal his punch until the proper opening develops. This is especially important in crowded or cramped situations where movement is limited, such as alleys, elevators, and hallways.

Sifu Royce Bunch demonstrates short power on two students using a large phone book, touching the phone book (left) and dropping palm (right).

Another important consideration when gauging a technique is simplicity. The technique should be as simple and as direct as possible from point of origin to point of impact. Short power fulfills this prerequisite nicely because it is a no-nonsense, no-frills type of strike. The movement is so short that from a distance it looks more like a touch than a strike. The strike almost seems to float toward the target, because the true power is hidden within the movement.

Third, the technique should be versatile. Short power can be used by any style or no style. It will take the qualities you already possess and make your best technique even better. It can be used with a variety of hand techniques, from fist to finger or from knuckle to palm. Its speed can be varied as well. When the strike is slow, the target will be propelled backward as the body attempts to escape from the shockwave created by the strike. If the strike is thrown quickly, it causes damage inside the target depending on the point struck. Short power becomes the medium through which your best techniques can be delivered.

And finally, a good technique should require little equipment so it can be practiced anywhere, anytime. Unlike many martial systems, it should be easily mastered and easily practiced. Short power effectively fulfills these requirements. A good technique should also exhibit strength, endurance, and speed.

The following training method may be used to develop short power. Practice twenty minutes per day or longer, every day or three days per week, depending on your schedule.

Long range

Medium range

Short range

Very short range

very short. Do not lean into the target; turn from the waist into the target. Hold a few minutes at each position, tense the whole body, then press to the point of shaking. At each of the four levels, go into the target in sequence and step backward in sequence. Remember to hold the tension at each level.

Section I: Strength and Endurance

Place a pillow or another soft object against a wall. Place your fist or palm against the target and push using four different ranges: long, medium, short, and

Section II: Progressive Resistance

Fill a sack with dried rice, beans, or corn. Start with weight you can lift with only your wrist, and increase weight periodically as you gain strength. Stand in the stance shown in the following photo, holding the neck of the sack. Inhale, then tense as you exhale and

Sifu Royce Bunch demonstrates wrist training.

Iron palm bag training

turn from the waist using only the wrist. Lift the bag and hold for one minute. Relax, then repeat several times.

Section III: Varying Distance and Tempo

Mount an iron palm bag to a wall or post. (Alternatively, you may use a punching bag.) Remember to put *dit da jow* lotion on your hands before training. Start with your hand one inch from the target. Rotate your waist and remain relaxed until impact. Upon contact, press into the target and exhale, shaking the hand on impact. At this level you can practice varying the speed—fast, slow, slow, fast. Work your way backward a few inches at a time, then work your way inward again.

Conclusion

These techniques will pay big dividends as long as you are consistent and persistent. You will be amazed at how hard you can punch after only six months of training. Work hard and your short power will take you a long way.

This material originally appeared in the January 1999 issue of Inside Kung-Fu.

2

Body by Billy Blanks

This Tournament Champion Proves You Don't Have to Be Lean to Be Mean in the Ring

Dave Cater

Billy Blanks once considered Bruce Lee the prototypical martial artist. In the legendary film star, Blanks saw a man who was quick and powerful despite a stature that would hardly strike the fear of God in a nun.

"I always thought a martial artist should be thin," Blanks recalls with a chuckle.

But five years ago, Blanks met a martial artist who believed that one didn't have to be lean to be mean. Cees Smith, a *judo* player from Holland, maintained that the proper weight-training program would only enhance the quickness and power of a fighter. Thin, he said, was definitely not in. "He said if I started working out I would be able to get off the line quicker. I would be bigger, faster, and most importantly, I would be able to explode off the line," Blanks noted.

Backed by his newfound training regimen, Blanks exploded onto the tournament point-fighting circuit and quickly became the man to beat. In 1983, he was a grand champion fighting staple and easily earned a number-one ranking.

However, Blanks's contribution to the martial arts goes beyond mere fighting technique. Through his success he has shown that a martial artist need not be held down by building up. By training for speed and endurance rather than bulk and size, the fighter can enjoy the best of both worlds. With the help of both famed bodybuilder Arnold Schwarzenegger and former Mr. Universe Mike Quinn, Blanks developed a personal workout program that generates explosive power. Subsequently, Blanks's opponents rarely see what they've been hit with.

"When I started weight lifting, I wanted to make sure my *karate* skills didn't diminish," said Blanks, who began martial arts training in 1970 in Erie, Pennsylvania. "I wanted to create both a power and

7

endurance workout. I wanted to make it more like circuit training." According to Blanks, training only for body bulk causes the martial arts fighter to "lock up" after throwing a combination of punches. The endurance factor, he noted, is nonexistent. In addition to training with weights four days per week, one and a half hours per day, Blanks also boxes for an hour and spends another three hours honing his martial arts skills.

Through weight work, Blanks went from 167 pounds in 1981 to 215 pounds in 1983. Another benefit came in the area of confidence. Knowing the training had made him quicker and stronger also made him mentally tougher in the ring.

"[Weight training] teaches you not to hesitate," said Blanks, a notorious first-puncher off the line. "It's the same as bench pressing, which also teaches you not to hesitate. Mentally, they work together. When you have 400 pounds on your chest, if you hesitate you get hurt. If you hesitate when you fight you get hit."

Blanks, who with his wife, Gayle, has two children (Shelly and Billy Jr.), said a weight program is especially beneficial in the off-season, when arm and leg muscles need time to rest.

"I try to take off two or three months and do different types of training," said Blanks, who lives in Quincy, Massachusetts. "Martial artists who train all year are just hurting themselves. I guarantee they'll have some type of elbow or knee problems. Weight training strengthens the damaged muscles while things like martial arts forms can develop different muscles."

Citing professional football and basketball players who study ballet and other sports during the downtime between seasons, Blanks noted that repeated use of injured areas will soon take its toll. "It's been a long time since I hurt a knee, leg, or shoulder," he added. "I attribute that to my weight training."

Billy Blanks has made a smooth transition from skinny martial artist to powerful tournament fighter. And he said he owes it all to his weight program. "It makes your body last longer and feel better. It enhances your speed and quickness, as well as your confidence in the ring."

Billy Blanks's Weight-Training Schedule

Exercise	Repetition	Weight used (pounds)
MONTE		

MONDAY (TOTAL WORKOUT TIME 1½ HOURS)
Benefits chest, shoulders, and triceps

Exercise	Repetition	Weight used (pounds)
Bench press	5 sets of 5	400–500
Incline press	5 sets of 5	400–500
Decline press	5 sets of 5	400–500
Cable fly	5 sets of 12	Work down from 80 per arm
Dumbell fly	5 sets of 12	Work down from 80 per arm
Pec deck	5 sets of 10	Start at 80 and work to 130
Pullover	5 sets of 10	80–85
Military press behind the neck	4 sets of 10	Start at 135 and work to 225
Upright row	4 sets of 10	Start at 135 and work to 185
Reverse pec deck for rear deltoids	5 sets of 10	160–170
Front and side laterals on cable machine	5 sets of 10 with each exercise	Start at 80, work up to 140, then go back down to 80

Exercise	Repetition	Weight used (pounds)

MONDAY (TOTAL WORKOUT TIME 1½ HOURS) (CONTINUED)
Benefits chest, shoulders, and triceps

Exercise	Repetition	Weight used (pounds)
Close-grip bench press	5 sets of 10	Start at 135 and work to 275
Reverse close-grip bench press	5 sets of 10	Start at 135
Behind-the-neck triceps press with cable machine	5 sets of 10	Start at 80, work to 140, and then go back to 80

TUESDAY (TOTAL WORKOUT TIME 1½ HOURS)
Benefits biceps and back

Exercise	Repetition	Weight used (pounds)
Bent-over row with dumbell	5 sets of 10	Start with 85 and work to 100
Seat row (machine)	5 sets of 10	Start with 120 and work to 240
Incline row	5 sets of 10	Start with 60 and work to 70
Lat pulldown	5 sets of 10	Start with 80, work to 140, then go back to 80
V-grip chin-ups	5 sets of 10	Bodyweight
Standing barbell curl	1 set of 10	25 pounds on each end; then as many sets of 10 as possible with weight added to each side
Seated dumbbell curl	5 sets of 10	No more than 60
Bent-over dumbbell curl	5 sets of 10	35

WEDNESDAY (TOTAL WORKOUT TIME 1½ HOURS)
Benefits legs

Exercise	Repetition	Weight used (pounds)
Seated calf raise	5 sets of 10	Warm up with 100; go to 235
Standing calf raise	5 sets of 10	Warm up with 100, go to 180
Donkey calf raise	5 sets of 10	With someone heavy on your back (you lift him)
Behind-the-neck squat	20 times each	Warm up at 135 and move up to 225, 325, and as high as possible up to 505
Hack squat	5 sets of 10	Up to 315
Leg extension	5 sets of 10	Go from heavy to middle to light weight (this will vary per individual)
Leg curl	5 sets of 10	Warm up with 80 and work up to 120
Walk the steps	Until you can't continue (this will vary per individual)	

THURSDAY—DAY OFF

FRIDAY—REPEAT MONDAY WORKOUT

Tale of the Tape

Name	Billy Blanks
Age	31
Home	Quincy, Massachusetts
Occupation	Martial arts school owner
Neck	18″
Biceps	18″
Triceps	18″
Thigh	26″
Waist	29″
Shoulders	46″
Forearm	16″
Calf	18″
Chest	48″
Reach	81″
Height	6′1″
Weight	215

Strength Training and Female Athletes

Charles I. Staley, M.S.S.

Traditionally, women have been reluctant to engage in resistance exercise for several reasons. First, many women fear the possibility of gaining significant amounts of body weight or developing male characteristics. This fear is reinforced when women see their mesomorphic peers in strength and power sports such as weight lifting, bodybuilding, and track-and-field throwing events.

An additional factor to consider is that women, by virtue of their high proportion of slow-twitch muscle fibers and low levels of the male hormone testosterone, are not inherently talented when it comes to strength performance. If you look around the next time you're in the gym, you'll see that most men concentrate on strength training, while most women focus on aerobic fitness and flexibility. After all, people tend to do what comes most easily to them and avoid the fitness components that really need the work.

Nevertheless, while men and women have more similarities than differences, there are eight key things to keep in mind if you're a woman looking to improve your strength preparation, or if you train women as a coach or trainer.

1. Compared to men, women often have hypermobile (overly loose) elbows and knees. Women who can hyperextend either their knees or elbows beyond 180 degrees should pay extra attention to the hamstrings and arm biceps (using leg curls and arm curls, respectively) in their weight-training program. Shortening these muscles will improve the stability and reduce the potential for injury at the elbow and knee.

2. Women generally have wider hips than men, which often increases tracking problems of the kneecap. In such cases, paying extra attention to the

vastus medialis muscle (the inner part of the quadriceps that helps to offset the usually stronger vastus lateralis) can go a long way toward alleviating knee pain and dysfunction. One remedy is the use of leg extensions, performed only at the last 10 to 20 degrees of extension. Well-designed equipment, such as machines made by Atlantis, provide built-in range-of-motion limiters for this purpose.

3. Although few women can gain appreciable muscle mass through weight training, it may surprise many to know that high reps may have the greatest potential to put muscle on the female body. This is because slow-twitch muscle (which most women have plenty of) responds best to endurance activities. If you've ever wondered why rowers and kayak racers have large back muscles despite large volumes of distance training, now you know the reason. Men or women who wish to get stronger without getting bigger are best served by low-repetition (two to three) sets. A word of caution, however: this type of training should only be considered after a significant period (one to two years) of work has been performed in the six- to twelve-repetition range.

4. Women who wear high heels are prone to excessively short calf muscles and tendons. Wearing heels prevents these structures from reaching their normal length, which, in turn, causes a compensatory shortening. If at all possible, bring a pair of low-heel shoes with you, so that you can switch back and forth during the day. In any event, calf stretching should be a high priority if you wear heels.

5. Eating disorders (and poor eating habits in general) appear to be at an all-time high among women in Western countries. If you are not eating enough calories (and particularly the right kind of calories), you simply will not have an adequate support mechanism for proper training. In my experience, women tend to eat too infrequently (I suggest five to six meals per day); and when they do eat, too many calories come from carbohydrates, and too few from fat and protein. On the other hand, women tend to do a better job with drinking enough water than men.

6. Women tend to enjoy (and, in my opinion, overdo) aerobic exercise, due to their high proportion of slow-twitch muscle. If you fit into this category, try to keep aerobic sessions as far away from strength sessions as possible—preferably on opposite days. If you feel you must do both during the same session, perform the strength component first.

7. Women tend to have better flexibility than men and spend a lot more time stretching than men. Unless you have a specific flexibility deficit, you're better off stretching after strength-training sessions, rather than before them. This is because most forms of stretching leave the muscle temporarily weaker, which will compromise your efforts in the weight room.

8. Because women tend to overemphasize aerobic exercise, they also tend to make strength sessions more like cardio sessions by emphasizing high reps and taking only short (and often incomplete) rests between sets. Remember that muscles get stronger by being exposed to high tensions, not by undergoing long workouts.

Finally, it's interesting to observe that as women's sports have become more popular and women have increased participation in martial arts, the performance differences between men and women have been narrowing. This may indicate that women are not as physiologically "inferior" to men as many have assumed, but that social and cultural factors are more to blame. With the recent popularity of women's professional boxing, basketball, and other sports, women are enjoying enhanced opportunities in athletic fields. It is hoped that this will lead to greater scientific research and technological advances in female athletic performance.

This material originally appeared in the July 1999 issue of Martial Arts Illustrated.

Increase Your Power—the Right Way

Done Correctly, a Bodybuilding Program Can Drastically Increase Your Speed, Power, and Strength

Robert Dreeben

In UFC 12 (the twelfth Ultimate Fighting Championship tournament), Vitor Belfort, a disciple of Gracie *jujitsu*, squares off against Scott Ferrozzo, who outweighs Belfort by well over 100 pounds. The fight begins, tension mounts, and in 52 seconds the match is over with Belfort as the victor. However, the battle was not won by the grappling finesse of Gracie *jujitsu*.

What took this man down was a quick succession of hard, fast, and strong punches to his head fueled by power and muscle. In this age in which grappling reigns supreme, let us not forget the effectiveness pure striking can have.

Today, so much research has been done in the area of physical human development that all the guesswork has been removed from physical training. Whatever your goals are, there are specific exercises and routines to achieve them.

For most martial artists, the goal is form with function. Obviously, what good are big or well-defined muscles if you can't use them combatively? In this article when I use the term *bodybuilding* I am referring to training with weights or resistance machines. Even if your goal only is to increase strength, progressive resistance exercises still build and enhance the body. Many readers get hung up on the term *bodybuilding*, thinking it is only training for physical enhancement. In reality, proper strength training often leads to aesthetic physical reshaping only as a fringe benefit.

As a student, researcher, and instructor, I have conferred with licensed trainers, nutritionists, and physicians regarding the science and application of bodybuilding. The principles in this chapter are based on pragmatic theory where results are measured in a laboratory setting. However, the universal concept of "no free lunch" is still the foundation of the truth: you get what you put in with interest.

Twenty-First-Century *Kung Fu*

Most martial arts systems were created hundreds of years ago. Even then most styles took a holistic approach by incorporating various auxiliary power and strength exercises into their martial package. So why add bodybuilding today? Because all those power exercises were developed before there was any such thing as gyms, spas, health clubs, or technology applied to strength development. We must realize that we can maintain the integrity of our style without being restrained in tradition.

Many of the ancient strength-training exercises are not only outdated but ineffective, and can be, in some cases, injurious to the body in the long term. If athletes today were stuck in the tradition and training methods of the past, they would not be surpassing the records of their Olympian forefathers. So why then have today's Olympic champions broken so many records? It's not because humans are getting better genetically. Rather, we are getting smarter, making new discoveries, and improving training technologies.

If you are a student of *kung fu* or *karate* who wants to stay in shape with the martial arts, then prepare to devote a lot of extra time in the *kwoon* or *dojo* to performing pushups, situps, and assorted calisthenics. Another misconception is that classical "complete" styles will keep you young and in the best of health. This is not always true. I could show you some older masters who are overweight, don't eat right, and are in poor health, but could still beat you senseless. The untimely passing of several of today's famous masters can serve as proof.

After years of proper training in the martial arts, you will attain a functional level of skill that is relatively low maintenance compared to when you first began. Physical sensitivity, improved timing, technique, and combat strategy compensate for and sur-

pass brute strength. But function is not always synonymous with health. Even with today's science and technology in bodybuilding, you still have to push your body to maximum intensity to achieve results.

If you are satisfied with maintaining what you have and like what you see in the mirror, then you have no reason to read further. You've got the answers, so skip to the next chapter. However, if you desire to reach your genetic potential, maintain youth and health, and develop more power and strength in your *kung fu*, the following principles will be of great benefit.

The Art and Science of Bodybuilding

With such a variety of weight-training routines, body-part splits, and so on, which is best? Experts still disagree about which are the best routines and theories. What is most important is how you implement the routine you choose and adapt it to your own body.

We must first distinguish between *muscle memory* and *muscle hypertrophy* (muscle enlargement accompanied by an increase in strength). To develop muscle memory, such as learning a *kung-fu* form, the nervous system needs constant repetition. Like making a path through the woods, the more you walk over it the better and clearer the path becomes. The more you repeat the movement, the better your nervous system memorizes the trigger patterns. Eventually you can run the form reflexively by "feeling" rather than "thinking."

Champion bodybuilder Mike Mentzer has based his "Heavy Duty" training method on the initial studies of Arthur Jones, the inventor of the Nautilus machines. With Mentzer's principle, less is more. He teaches that muscular growth beyond normal levels is related to intensity of effort rather than continual repetitions. One set, performed with maximum effort that leads to muscular failure, is enough to trigger the mechanisms in the body that cause anabolic muscle growth. Any further repetitions past this point with a heavy weight do not increase growth, but rather are counterproductive and lengthen the road to recovery.

Since Mentzer started teaching his Heavy Duty routine years ago, he has made new discoveries and adaptations. Many famous trainers today use their own interpretation of his system without giving him credit. In his tapes and seminars, Mentzer always states, "A bodybuilding session should not be a muscle endurance workout." He also teaches that the amount of or lack of muscle soreness is not an indicator of how much work you've done or what gains you will achieve. In fact, the application of deep massage right after a workout can minimize a good portion of work-related muscle pain and enhance recovery.

Wisdom of the Body

"I train and train but still don't see results." This is a common and frustrating complaint. The body basically runs on a preprogrammed automatic pilot, and we encounter problems because these programs were formatted in prehistoric times.

For instance, after an injury the body can regenerate most of its systems. Even internal organs perforated from gunshot wounds can heal with a little help from surgeons. But when spinal cord injuries occur, the body refuses to regenerate it. It's like the body says, "The injury is too immobilizing. Here in the wild you'll get eaten or die of starvation before healing would make you mobile again, so it's not even worth trying to heal." Today, scientists are striving to develop new drugs that countermand this program and force regeneration.

Knowledge and implementation of principles that supersede the prehistoric program are what it takes for you to maintain a state of continual improvement and break through training plateaus that prevent you from reaching your genetic potential. For instance, despite our intense training, our body's survival program would rather maintain a higher level of body fat and less muscle mass. Our desire for optimal performance is not relevant; in fact, it is contrary to the prehistoric program. In times of famine, the body is able to feed off its fat stores.

We know the benefits of lowering body fat and increasing lean mass. The body, on the other hand, does not. The more muscle you have, the more food you need to maintain it, and becoming higher maintenance is contrary to the body's reflexive systems. Fat is easy to maintain. This is why after you've trained your body to be fat (by overeating), simply dieting will not always get rid of the extra fat. It takes much less food to maintain the fat than it did to put it there in the first place.

This is where "fat-burning" cardio work comes in, and this is why many people have a hard time achieving the results they want. In our quest for improvement we are fighting against the body's end-gaining wisdom.

Because of this "fixed maintenance" program, the physical structure will not change unless it's forced to. Through our training methods of continual adaptive exercise, we slowly reprogram and upgrade our biological software. In other words, "constructive destruction."

As we get older our bodies start to weaken and degenerate. Theoretically, barring severe genetic "time bomb" defects, the continually improving athlete will have fortified his or her system to a point of health that will compensate for and slow the aging process, and will therefore look and feel better than a sedentary counterpart.

How Not to Exercise

In our typical martial arts workout, most of us have to avoid a select group of movements or techniques because of old injuries. Or, if an injury is not present, a particular movement might be avoided because it is just not right for one's body structure. Certain styles are generally not suited for older students (fifty years of age and up)—specifically, *wushu*, savate, monkey style, and *capoiera*. Even the high kicks of the relatively benign art of *Tae Kwon Do* can easily give an older person a compressed disc if he's not careful. Through time, practice, and deepening sensitivities to our bodies, we can usually tell whether a new movement will be harmful. In bodybuilding this is not always the case.

In this section, John Boos offers training tips to enhance performance and avoid injuries. Boos, a former pro bodybuilder, is also a certified professional exercise instructor with over thirty years in the health and fitness field. He is also a licensed massage therapist and advanced sports massage therapist. He designs and constructs his own fitness machines that adapt to your body (rather than your having to adapt to the machine).

Boos's clients come from all walks of life—from physicians and bodybuilders to martial artists and Olympic athletes. He instructs his clients, young and old, male and female, in the "*kung fu*" of bodybuilding.

The lat machine is a popular piece of equipment found in almost all gyms and health clubs. Unfortunately, many people are practicing a harmful variation of pulling the bar behind the neck.

"The lat pulldown should never be done behind the back. Range of motion is restricted; you have the humerus being laterally rotated to its absolute end point, which is the most dangerous place to put the joint," Boos explains. "Any joint in any exercise at its end point is a dangerous point to train."

A similar situation exists with the shoulder press behind the neck with the barbell. "There is nothing we do in life that can simulate the press behind the neck or the lat machine pulldown behind the neck," Boos notes.

In bodybuilding there are less obvious ways to injure the shoulders. One is the steep incline bench press. The incline bench press allegedly works your upper pectorals—"allegedly" because it has still not been proven medically that incline causes any deeper contraction of the upper pectorals than either the flat bench or decline. According to Boos, "The steeper the incline, the more and more the shoulder starts to compensate for the pecs."

Personally, when I do an incline press, I use the Smith machine with the backrest adjusted with a very slight 20-degree incline for variation. Most fixed incline benches use a steep incline, which starts to use more deltoid and less pec. This angle, when you go heavy, can overstress the shoulders. "If you want to do shoulders, then do shoulders correctly," Boos insists.

Incline dumbbell flyes are another popular self-destructive exercise seen in many gyms. "Probably the worst exercise for your shoulders would be the incline dumbbell fly," Boos notes. "Always use a flat

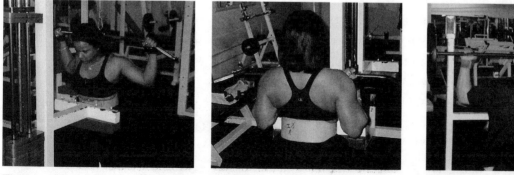

The lat pulldown should never be done behind the neck (left). The correct method is to pull down to the front of the chest (right).

Bad form: A shoulder press should never be done behind the neck. The correct method is to press in front of the chest.

The worst exercise for your shoulders is the incline dumbbell fly. The flat bench (right) is a safer alternative.

A safer exercise for the incline is on the Smith machine with only a 20-degree incline.

Never roll your shoulders while performing a shoulder shrug. Here, the author shrugs 200 pounds.

bench." Other exercises Boos warns against are "bent-over barbell rows without a chest support. Don't even go near it. There's no way you can statically hold your lower back in that position with a weight that is capable of working your lats to any effectiveness. Never do a pullup behind the neck and never roll your shoulders while performing a shoulder shrug."

Optimum Power

This is where concentration, form, and technique come together. I cannot overemphasize the importance of maintaining proper form and posture while performing various weight-lifting exercises. Next is to use a slower lifting speed. According to Boos, "Many trainees move too fast, jerking the weight using inertia rather than pure strength." He recommends a three-three protocol: three-second concentric (raising), then three-second eccentric (lowering) motion. Coordinate your breathing (don't forget to breathe), exhaling when raising and inhaling when lowering.

Include creative visualization. Just like punching through the target, focus past the point where you are struggling to the point of full extension. For advanced training, you can add dynamic tension to certain exercises that allow for it. For example, when doing the pec deck, upon bringing the arms

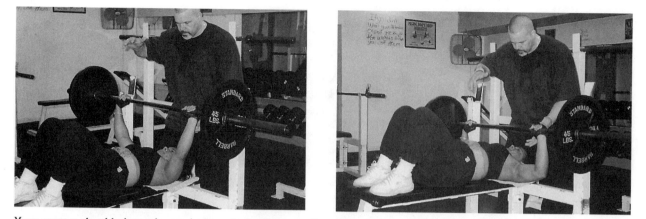

Your spotter should always be ready to assist in the same direction you are pressing. Here, 135 pounds is being pressed.

together, pause and with dynamic tension increase the contraction for a three-count. After one set you will feel like you've done twenty sets.

A complete exercise program should add specific exercises that enhance the full range of muscle functionality. Explosive movement is one action of functional strength that is of great use to the martial artist. One of my favorite adaptive variations of the bench press imitates the full range of muscular action.

Begin with 135 pounds on the bar (that's one 45-pound plate on each side and a 45-pound bar). This is normally my warm-up weight. Press up to full extension. Now lower the bar slowly, taking six seconds to reach your chest. Stop the bar one inch from your chest and pause for three seconds. Then press upward explosively, as fast and as hard as you can. Repeat the sequence. The first one to three reps actually feel easy. By six I'm struggling. Seven or eight would be total failure, but I push myself to ten reps with the help of my spotter. This exercise is metaphysical. You expand the mind by exceeding the so-called limits of the body while you embrace and transcend the boundaries of pain.

This exercise variation is one example in which a fast lifting speed would be appropriate. Your best muscle- and strength-building results will come when your body says, "Seven reps are all I can do," but your strength of spirit and willpower forces your

Using a slower lifting speed, such as a three-second curl in each direction, will work the muscle more than a fast jerk that uses inertia.

body to perform two or three more. You can do it if you try, and this will increase your concentration and focus to the mind/body connection.

Understanding more of the *kung fu* in bodybuilding, Boos offers some fine points of general lifting technique. Concerning pulling actions, he notes, "Another thing I see with pulldowns, pullups, and seated cable rows, is they let their shoulders relax when they go out to full protraction or full extension. Keep your shoulders loaded, keep your biceps slightly loaded. You don't ever want to relax your biceps, elbow joint, or shoulders.

"By keeping it loaded, you are keeping the synergy muscles intact, keeping the joints in their proper place. If you relax, the synergists are going to have to re-load up," he adds. "This will cause a lot of instability in the joint. When you couple that relaxation with the sloppy protocol of moving too fast, now you have a tugging effect that can lead to injury."

Conclusion

Incorporating stretching and massage in conjunction with your workout will help greatly reduce injuries and shorten the road to recovery. Between sets you can stretch the particular muscle group you are working. This helps stimulate growth and maintain flexibility. Massage during or immediately after your workout increases circulation and minimizes muscle soreness.

Drink plenty of water during and after your sessions to stay hydrated. Always maintain a straight and balanced posture and movement, visualizing *chi* flow. Remember, if you continue to do what you have always been doing, you will continue to get the same results (or non-results). If you want change, then you must change your attitude, thought pattern, and physical methods.

This material originally appeared in the April 1999 issue of Inside Kung-Fu.

PART 2

Endurance Training

Martial Arts—Aerobic or Anaerobic?

Debora Toole Sommerville

After extensive research working with different disciplines in the martial arts industry, I have found that combative and competitive styles train with a combination of aerobic and anaerobic exercise. To be more specific, training drills that include focus pad work, bag work, and continuous sparring are considered anaerobic. Conditioning drills such as jumping rope, air punching and kicking, and road work are considered aerobic. With this concept in mind, a martial arts practitioner needs nutritional supplementation to provide the body with proper recovery.

Let me explain a little more about the meaning of *aerobic* and *anaerobic*, the body's two primary systems that supply energy. With aerobic exercise, oxygen is required to provide energy for the activity. The body needs energy to live and function. This aerobic system uses carbohydrates and fat for energy, but predominantly fat, which is why it can deliver so much energy for so long. Fat stores can last almost indefinitely; it's the carbohydrates that are in short supply. We burn about one calorie per minute of fat when in a resting state. Since there are 3,500 calories in one pound of fat, sitting around is not a good way of trying to get rid of excess fat. Nevertheless, we are in the aerobic state when at rest and burning predominantly fat.

Working at a Faster Pace

To stay in the aerobic state, and thus burn as much fat as possible, we must gradually speed up this at-rest state so we have more muscles working and at a faster pace. This demands more oxygen, which consequently burns more fat, which is why you start breathing harder when you start exercising. Now, as long as you can satisfy the working muscles' need for oxygen, then you are still basically in the aerobic state, predominantly burning fat and certainly much faster than when in a resting state.

So ideally, you want to slowly speed your body up to its last true "steady state." In this state, if you increased the exercise intensity, you would not be able to supply enough oxygen to meet the working muscles' needs, and the body would have to go to another energy system to try to meet the demand.

The alternative energy system runs only on carbohydrates and can't get rid of its waste products very quickly, so it doesn't last very long. You have crossed the *anaerobic threshold*. This threshold is certainly crossed before you reach maximum effort. So, the place just before you reach this threshold is what we call the last "true steady" state of the body—a place that we can stay in a long time and burn the greatest amount of fat in the least amount of time.

A good rule of thumb here is what we call *perceived exertion*. The intensity is such that you are breathing significantly harder than at rest, and you can still talk but probably are unable to say full sentences while performing your aerobic exercise. This could be anywhere from 65 to 85 percent of maximum heart rate (MHR).

Crossing the Threshold

Skeletal muscles can produce energy even when the cardiovascular system is unable to deliver oxygen to the working muscles to meet their energy needs. When this happens, you cross the anaerobic threshold and the anaerobic energy system takes over. So, naturally, *anaerobic* means "without oxygen." The muscles are now producing energy without oxygen. We burn very little fat while doing anaerobic exercise.

Anaerobic energy relies mostly on carbohydrates. When producing energy anaerobically—such as with weight training, sprinting, or sparring—your muscles eventually stop working due to a buildup of lactic acid, which is the by-product of producing energy without oxygen. (The lactic acid is what causes the burning sensation you feel in your muscles.) As you recall, when the muscles don't have to work as hard (such as when jogging, jumping rope, or riding a bike), you are producing energy with oxygen (inhaling) and the by-products (water and carbon dioxide) are easily expended (exhaling).

Unfortunately, but fortunately, when lactic acid builds up during anaerobic exercise, it stops the muscles from working by changing the chemical climate in the muscle cells. The fortunate part is that this is the body's way of telling you to stop before you tear something. When you stop and rest, your body begins to clear the lactate and convert it back to pyruvate to make energy available once more in the muscle cell so you can continue to exercise. This is why you have to rest between sets when you lift, and why you have to stop and catch your breath between sprints or rounds of sparring.

Anaerobic exercise uses very little fat and relies on stored carbohydrates (glycogen) in the muscles for its energy. It is important to have a good meal with lots of carbohydrates anywhere from one and a half to three and a half hours before you train anaerobically. A small snack of fruit is also beneficial about forty-five minutes prior to training. If you train first thing in the morning, have a meal replacement drink about forty-five minutes to one hour before you work out. The drink is already partially predigested and will be in your system much sooner than whole food. Now your anaerobic energy system will be fully charged for your workout.

Burning Body Fat

Even though it is true we do not really burn fat during anaerobic exercise, it is also true that anaerobic training burns many calories and increases the body's fat-burning capacity by adding more muscle. Fat is only burned in the muscle, so the more muscle you have working, the more fat you will burn. Anaerobic exercise significantly increases your metabolic rate not only by the addition of new muscle, but by greatly increasing the body's overall need for calories. Every reaction in the body requires energy for the reaction to take place, and energy uses calories. Therefore, after anaerobic training, during recovery time, your body is building new muscle, and this uses calories. The newly rebuilt muscle is now larger, requiring even more calories to support it. If all your calories are not supplied by food, the body will take what it needs from your fat stores when all variables are properly controlled. Therefore, anaerobic training can be an effective way of assisting in reducing fat stores. When combined properly with aerobic training, it is the fastest, most effective way to reduce your fat stores.

When your goal is to build or maintain lean body mass and lose fat, do your anaerobic training first while glycogen stores are full. Proceed immediately to your aerobic workout while your heart rate is already elevated. Martial arts training is a combination of aerobic and anaerobic exercise. Depending on the instruction, students can achieve optimum strength, speed, and endurance through proper organization of class instruction. Deplete glycogen stores in the beginning of class. Stretch out the full body and then proceed to the isometric or resistance exercises (bag work, pushups, punching combination, or kicking drills). Then go on to the endurance training and road work (aerobic). You will develop your mean fighting machine—the human body!

This material originally appeared in the March 1999 issue of Inside Kung-Fu.

Building Your Endurance
Supercircuit Training for Martial Arts

Jimmie Nixdorf

Martial arts training requires a great deal of learning. Once you have learned the basic techniques, you will soon learn their applications through such exercises as forms and sparring. In free sparring, one vital concept to learn is energy conservation.

Without a doubt, you will discover that operating in the ring under totally spontaneous conditions can make you really tired really fast. And since everything you learn in the training hall provides representative results for what you may experience in the outside world, imagine how winded you can get in a street encounter, when twenty seconds can seem like an eternity.

To master energy conservation in free sparring or self-defense, you must work on your aerobic endurance. It has been suggested that one who can't breathe can't fight either; therefore, training your body to respond under trying conditions can be nothing but beneficial for you. One such method of training your body to adapt itself aerobically is *supercircuit conditioning*.

Supercircuit conditioning is a type of cross-training that allows you to alternate running with other exercises to develop your cardiovascular system along with your muscle groups to holistically condition yourself. Supercircuit conditioning is not only used by many cross-trainers, but also by some military groups, police academies, and similar organizations to promote job-related skills. Likewise, supercircuit training can have its advantages for the martial arts practitioner.

How Does It Work?

Supercircuit training develops your aerobic and muscular fitness by combining running with various calisthenic exercises over a set time period. You begin by running for one minute. At the end of the minute, you do another exercise, such as pushups, for a one-minute period, and resume running after that minute has elapsed. You may interweave several different types of calisthenics with running to promote your physical fitness.

Say, for example, that you perform a supercircuit conditioning routine for nine minutes in a given workout. A possible routine for these nine minutes could be as follows:

1. Begin with running
2. Pushups
3. Running
4. Stomach crunches
5. Running
6. Jumping jacks
7. Running
8. Pushups
9. Running

Whether you choose to go for an odd or even amount of minutes, you should begin and end with running. It is easier to alternate exercises for one minute apiece if you perform for an odd amount of minutes, but if you do choose to run for an even amount, then your last running session will be two minutes in duration.

You may perform all different calisthenic exercises, or you may repeat an exercise as many times as you wish. If you do choose to repeat exercises within a given routine, you will notice that you are able to do fewer each time you repeat the exercise; however, keep striving to do all you can within the minute. You will be working toward muscular failure the more time you spend performing the routine, but the more you practice supercircuit conditioning, the sooner your body will become more aerobically fit to perform feats under pressure. And if you perform these exercises individually, apart from the supercircuit routine, improvement in your physical ability to perform may arise.

Alternating Exercises

The exercises you intermingle with your running can add a great deal of intensity to your supercircuit conditioning program. You may alternate exercises to build your strength, increase your flexibility, or continue developing your cardiovascular endurance. You may even get a sense of using your fighting skills by incorporating your techniques into the supercircuit session. Consider the following examples of some exercises you may use.

Pushups strengthen your chest and triceps. They may be performed military style, clapping, or any other way you see fit. These will greatly assist you in the execution of hand strikes.

Abdominal work may take the form of leg lifts, stomach crunches, bicycles, and so on. Abdominal work will assist you in controlling your breathing, and it will help you to absorb blows received during sparring.

Frog hops may be used to further condition your cardiovascular system, as well as to condition your legs for kicking. To perform frog hops, begin in a squatting position and leap upward, extending your whole body upward. Because there is a great deal of cardiovascular work involved with frog hops, you probably won't want to perform more than one set during a given supercircuit session.

The **bionic man** exercise requires continuous motion, but it allows you a rest period of sorts during the exercise. Swing an arm straight upward while lifting the opposite knee. Then take a step, similar to marching in place, raising your other arm. When your right arm goes up, so too will your left knee, and vice versa. Continue this exercise, alternating at your own pace.

Pumpers are like standing crunches. In a standing position, place your hands behind your head. Then raise a knee and try to touch it with the elbow of your opposite arm, and continue alternating at your own pace. Like the bionic man exercise, pumpers can give you a degree of rest until it's time to run again.

These are just a few of many exercises you may perform during a supercircuit session. You can vary the calisthenic routines during a session, and receive different benefits with each set or session. Even the running may be varied, such as running backward or sideways, for a one-minute period. You are limited only by your own imagination as far as how a session is conducted, and it can be educational and fun to experiment.

Conducting a Session

Now that you have been exposed to a variety of ways to conduct a supercircuit session, the next step is to get out there and do it. But you should have some preparation prior to beginning the session.

A repeating timer is an essential piece of equipment during a supercircuit session. You don't want to have to worry about someone forgetting to reset the timer each time you stop to perform a different exercise.

Another factor to consider is the location of the session. Ideally you should exercise outdoors, but weather conditions and lack of privacy can sometimes hinder the workout. Supercircuit conditioning may be performed inside, though space is sometimes confining. But then again, you could run in place if necessary.

The size of the group training can be an important consideration. A smaller group may require less space than a larger group, especially if you're exercising by yourself. But for a larger group, you can try this running variation: have everyone run a single line, at different intervals; the person at the end of the line sprints forward to become the leader, and can change the pace of the run.

Finally, and possibly most important, decide how long you want the session to last. Sessions should include both a warm-up and cool-down period, and you should slow down if you feel yourself becoming too fatigued. Perform within your own limits, and gradually increase your time as you adapt to the sessions. The more you can increase your time, the better off you'll be when you need the proverbial quick blast of energy. But try not to overdo it in the first few sessions. After all, if you were in such superb physical condition, there would be no need for you to participate in any form of the supercircuit sessions.

Conclusion

Supercircuit conditioning may be used as infrequently as once a week, or as often as every day. And the beauty of the sessions is that through varying them by time, exercises, or other variables, you get different benefits each time you participate.

Supercircuit conditioning does not benefit your cardiovascular and muscular systems alone. For example, the supercircuit sessions are good for burning fat and toning your muscle mass, which can help you achieve weight-loss goals.

One of the primary areas that the supercircuit sessions condition is your mind. If you can keep up with a series of exercises for a given amount of time, then your self-discipline and determination are to be applauded. This exercise tests your perseverance, and can readily discern the winners from the losers by showing who will be quicker to quit. By pushing you to the limits, the session prepares you for the fight in the ring or on the street, because in such situations you may not get the opportunity to stop and catch your breath. On the street, falling by the wayside due to losing your breath can result in unacceptable losses.

By training in supercircuit conditioning, you can profoundly affect the quality of your training, as well as the quality of your life. With this in mind, you can gain a great deal simply by setting aside a few minutes for the combination of exercises to create a whole greater than the sum of its parts.

This material originally appeared in the April 1997 issue of Inside Karate.

Bruce Lee's Running Route

John R. Little

I've been involved in weight training and body-building for well over ten years. Over the years, I've interviewed every top bodybuilder and strength athlete in the business—from Mr. Olympia winners Arnold Schwarzenegger, Dorian Yates, and Lee Haney to the late Olympic weight-lifting champion Paul Anderson, a man considered by many people to have been the strongest man who ever lived.

Being around such paragons of strength and muscle, I came to accept the beliefs that abound within bodybuilding circles indicating that weight training will benefit all aspects of an athlete's game. To a large extent, this is certainly accurate. However, the one area in which weight training does not hold much sway is endurance. Granted, you can use light weights and circuit-train, which will provide some aerobic effect, but this is a very inefficient way to obtain aerobic fitness when compared to such

tried and true (and far more efficacious) methods as cross-country skiing or running.

Anyway, to my point. Not that long ago I lived in California and, as it happened, perhaps ten minutes away from Bruce Lee's old house on Roscomare Road in Bel Air. In the course of researching this book I was privileged to speak with many individuals who had the good fortune of training alongside Bruce Lee, such as NBA legend Kareem Abdul-Jabbar. Kareem particularly waxed euphoric about Lee's "incredible aerobics program" and their old running route on Roscomare Road: "Bruce and I used to start most of our workouts by running from his house on Roscomare Road out to Mulholland and back. It was a distance of about two miles and, because of the hills, it was a killer on the legs and cardiovascular system."

With Kareem's words ringing in my ears, I decided that I would get up early one morning, take a drive up past Bruce's old house, park the car, and go for a little jog. You know, just for sentimental value—in addition to testing the accuracy of ole Kareem's recollective faculty. After all, I reasoned, I'd been lifting weights for almost sixteen years; was strong as a bull from "Power Factor Training," a bodybuilding method that I'd cocreated with Peter Sisco; and my cardiovascular system was (or so I reasoned at the time) more than a match for such a piddly little two-mile trek. At least that was my mind-set as I started out on my nostalgic bit of early morning road work.

It was very early into the run when I realized I'd missed the side of the proverbial barn by at least eight yards in my estimation of my fitness levels. My body started sending none-too-subtle signals to my brain that I was not nearly in the kind of condition that I'd foolishly thought I was. I learned a lot about Bruce that morning—that he was evidently quite into hills, as Roscomare Road is loaded with them! And by hills I'm not talking about little bumps in the asphalt, but inclines that, at times, make Gibraltar look like an anthill!

As I continued pounding away, I noticed that my legs were now burning from lactic acid buildup—I'd misjudged the tempo I needed to employ to pace myself for this distance and at this intensity. After what seemed an eternity, I made my way up to the summit of a (painfully) steep hill that—finally!—intersected Mulholland Drive, the "turnaround point," according to Kareem.

At this point, my heart was pounding like a jackrabbit's as I turned around and continued back toward Bruce's house. Down the steep decline I went, then over a brief stretch of level pavement, before yet another steep hill reared up before me—another obstacle to overcome! I found the hills on the return trip were even more brutal than when I'd first crossed over them, and I found myself slowing down with each succeeding step until I finally ended up walking the remainder of the route.

I finally made it back to Bruce's house and then back to the comfort of my van. I opened the door and flopped down on the driver's seat, breathing like a racehorse and watching a pool of sweat form on the floor beneath me.

A Lesson from Brandon Lee

I realized then and there the validity of a point made to me by Brandon Lee during an interview I'd conducted with him shortly after he had finished his fourth feature film, *Rapid Fire*. We'd been discussing various training approaches and eventually got around to the subject of cardiovascular conditioning and its utility in day-to-day encounters, as opposed to training solely for strength and power.

"I've always done a lot of cardiovascular work because it's 'real world' power," Brandon explained. "I mean, I suppose having large muscles from weight training is good if you want to pick up heavy objects, but cardiovascular stamina is something that seems to come in handy a lot more often than large muscle would. I mean, if you go down to the Inosanto Academy [where Brandon was training in the martial arts] and you try and do a three-minute round on the Thai pads—I don't care how big your muscles are, if you don't have a good cardiovascular system, you're going to be dead in about forty-five seconds and I'm still going to be going."

Brandon had a point, I remember thinking to myself (in between gasps) after having just completed his father's old running route. Indeed, I was practically "dead," but I could well imagine Brandon's superbly conditioned father blowing past my pathetic-looking excuse for a runner on this very same road—with energy to burn!

I retained a sharp image of this in my mind as I drove the van back toward Mulholland Drive and, en route, discovered an interesting fact: the route that Bruce and Kareem (and now I) had jogged was only three-quarters of a mile each way—a total of only a mile and a half. Not a huge distance by any stretch, but then, if the intensity (as provided by the hills) is adequate, you really don't need a huge volume of such training to elicit a dramatic cardiovascular response. I recalled Bruce Lee's point regarding the nature of cardiovascular adaptation: "The other way [to train one's cardiovascular system] is progression; you must start out slow and then gradually build speed as your conditioning improves."

In other words, such training has to be progressive, and intensity (the difficulty of the exercise) is a factor that can be altered on a progressive basis through a process of either adding weight to your limbs while you run or by increasing the grade upon which you are running. The Roscomare route is obviously an example of the latter. (Although Bruce's training diaries revealed that he also did a form of double-progressive running by adding up to fifteen pounds of resistance to his limbs while he was running these hills!)

I should mention that the point of cardiovascular exhaustion that I reached in front of Bruce Lee's house on Roscomare Road that day was my starting point in revamping my beliefs toward training for total fitness. From that moment I implemented jogging as an adjunct to my own training, employing Bruce's principles of progression. And guess what? Last week I tried the old Roscomare route again and, with a better head toward pacing and a more seasoned cardiovascular system, I found that I was now able to complete the route without feeling like I'd just gone ten rounds with Bruce himself.

Cardiovascular conditioning is a wonderful tool, and not just for martial artists but for anyone who wishes to become healthier. Just as Bruce Lee taught us that a "style" or method of doing something automatically imposes limitations and represents at best a segment of a totality, no one training component holds all the answers to total conditioning.

Experiment with Bruce Lee's training methods and find that "sweet spot"—that perfect combination of endurance, strength, and flexibility training that will result in your achieving total fitness and optimum health and becoming the absolute best that you can be. Don't fall into the fitness trap that I and others before me have fallen into—allowing your five senses to atrophy while you search blindly for a so-called "sixth sense." Apply the teachings of Bruce Lee to your training; be your own investigating agent, and you'll be a far healthier person for doing so.

As a postscript, I should mention that I bumped into Kareem Abdul-Jabbar again, this time during a taping of a "Biography" television episode about Bruce Lee for the Arts and Entertainment Network. "Hey Kareem," I called out, "I tried out the old running route you told me about when you used to train with Bruce."

Kareem didn't even have to wait to hear the rest of my sorry tale to figure out what the inevitable result would have been. He just looked over and then flashed me a Cheshire cat grin. "Man, it kicked your ass, didn't it?"

Like the old proverb says, "There are no truer words than those born of experience."

This material originally appeared in the February 1996 issue of Martial Arts Legends.

PART 3

Flexibility Training

The Best of Modern and Ancient Stretching Methods

Thomas Kurz

You can have your splits in a matter of a few months or even weeks and then display them without any warm-up! All it takes is the right stretching method. If you spend a year or more on achieving a side split and still can't do it without warm-up, it means that the stretching method you use is incorrect, or you are chronically fatigued, or both.

Developing the ability to do splits is one of the easiest tasks in athletic training. If done right, it takes little time and effort. Why, then, do so many people spend hours weekly, year after year, and get such meager results? There are several reasons.

- *The wrong stretches.* No matter how hard you work, if you do wrong stretches, or have poor body alignment in your stretches, the results will be disappointing.

- *The wrong sequence of efforts.* If you use the wrong sequence of efforts (exercises) in a workout or in a set of consecutive workouts, it may double or triple your recovery time. You should do each exercise when it has the greatest effect.
- *The wrong training load.* Training loads that are too great without enough rest cause chronic fatigue. If you begin your workout still sore after the previous one, you are asking for an injury or at least hampering your progress.

Although front and side splits do not develop kicking ability or skills, they are of use to kickers. The straddle stance, which may eventually get so low that it becomes a side split, strengthens adductor muscles at their maximal range of motion. Strongly tensing muscles as they are being stretched (which is the essence of isometric stretching) causes these muscles to grow longer by adding sarcomeres in muscle fibers. Greater strength and length of the muscles, especially adductors of the supporting leg, prevent groin strains of that supporting leg when kicking or when that leg is swept.

For most people, the front split is easier to achieve than the side split because most have stronger and better-stretched hamstrings and hip flexors (iliopsoas muscles) than adductors (inner thigh muscles). Your ability to do the front split has little to do with the ability to do the side split.

The muscles you need to stretch to do the front split are buttocks, hamstrings, calves, and hip flexors. The muscles you need to stretch to do the side split are hip adductors and, to some degree, hip flexors. Also, the ligaments of the hip joint that restrict mobility in the front split and in the side split are different. In the front split it is the diofemoral ligament that restricts the amount of the thigh extension (how flat the rear leg lies on the ground).

In the side split, adduction of the thigh is restricted by the pubofemoral ligament. To relax the iliofemoral ligament while doing the front split, tilt your pelvis forward. To relax all ligaments, and particularly the pubofemoral ligament, while doing the side split, you also need to tilt the pelvis forward.

Side splits are not difficult. Anybody with normal range of motion in the joints of the hips and lower back can do them after learning the correct thigh-pelvis alignment and a little strength training of the adductors.

Weakness of the adductors is the main obstacle to doing side splits. Weak adductors cannot support your weight as you increase the angle between your thighs. The weak adductors are forced to tense beyond their capability, and they can be hurt or strained. Strong adductors can support you with less tension, pain, and resistance while you spread your legs all the way sideways to put your inner thighs on the floor. Generally, the stronger the muscle, the fewer motor units are recruited to support any given load.

Stronger muscles support you with less tension and pain. If your adductors are strong but you are not able to do the splits, it may be that nervous regulation of their length is set at less than their actual length. In that case, when you spread your legs, even in positions in which no weight is placed on them, your adductors will tense and not let you move beyond a certain point. In such cases, the only thing you need to do is to reset their nervous regulation. You can do it by practicing the classical horse stance or using isometric stretches, which are based on current knowledge of neurology and physiology.

Horse Stance: The Ancient Method

The *horse stance* (or *straddle stance*; *kiba dachi* in *karate*) is related to stretching. If you practice it at gradually increased depths (lowering hips more and more) and then widths (feet wider apart) you will eventually reach full straddle split. But before that, you will build impressive strength in your inner thigh muscles and be able to use that strength in a stretched position. You will also learn the most efficient way of aligning your pelvis, hip joints, and knees for splits and high side kicks.

Having problems with splits is typical for those who have received poor instruction or fail to set up a proper base as beginners, because proper training for beginners involves standing for several minutes in increasingly low stances, mainly in bow stance (*zenkutsu dachi* in *karate*) and horse stance (*kiba dachi*). Before beginners receive the first white belt in *karate*, they should be able to stand five minutes in a *kiba dachi* at least two shoulders wide. This makes them strong enough for further training and forces them to align the hips and legs just right for side splits and side kicks.

The horse stance remains a fundamental exercise of the Chinese martial arts and Okinawan and Japanese *karate*. Many systems have it because it is useful in actual fighting and as a tool of building leg strength, leg muscle endurance, flexibility, correct breathing, and patience.

Regardless of the system, the correct horse stance has these common features: weight is equally distributed on both legs, feet are at least shoulder-width apart, thighs are parallel to the ground, hips are low and relaxed, toes point forward or slightly inward, knees are slightly inward and not protruding past the toes, and the upper body is kept straight with the chest out.

The differences among systems are in hand position and width of stance. Some keep hands clenched in fists and placed at the waist; others keep them open and below the navel, palms up one over the other, or move open hands as if punching. In some, feet are half one's body length apart; in others, three times one's foot length apart; and in others, the distance is measured in steps, each step being a twist of both feet. In the latter case, starting from a position/stance "on attention," the first step is to move heels apart while toes stay together and the second step is to turn both feet on their heels so the toes point outward. Each odd step ends with toes pointing in, each even step with toes pointing out. The horse stance in such a system is done with feet an odd number of steps apart—for example, three, five, or seven.

Why should the toes point in? Because it works better in fighting! Today orthopedic surgeons know that keeping feet pointed in or at least forward in the same direction as the knees reduces stress on the medial meniscus and thus the likelihood of having it torn.

Why should the hips be low? So the upper body is kept straight and the chest is thrust out. Why? To relax the muscles of the abdomen and make it easy for the diaphragm to move freely when you breathe abdominally. Another reason is that in the low horse stance you tense your abductors (muscles outside your hips and buttocks), which causes the muscles that oppose them—adductors—to relax and thus make it easier to spread your feet wider. This neurological mechanism is called *reciprocal inhibition*.

Isometric Stretches: The Modern Method

Modern method is based on the knowledge of the mechanism of *postcontractive reflex depression*, and the effect of isometric or eccentric tension on stretched muscles, as well as the role of the pubofemoral and ischiofemoral ligaments of the hip joint.

Most people reach full side split with isometric stretching in one to six months. All it takes is to do these stretches two or four times per week, at the end of your regular workouts, preferably after weight lifting. Do not work out when you are sore or very tired. Both isometrics and lifting weights are strength exercises, and should be done during the same workout (strength workout).

The stretches are very simple: first, assume your initial position. For example, in the horse stance, tense the muscles to be stretched (in this case your inner thigh muscles) as hard as you can, relax them, and immediately increase the stretch (in this case, spread your legs wider). When you reach your current stretch limit, stand tensing the stretched muscles for a few seconds. This makes them stronger in this extended position. (Initial position for a front split will be standing with one leg in front, the other behind you, both on the same line; for the side split stand with legs spread more than shoulder-width apart.) You will be able to do splits with no warm-up when you easily stand for more than a minute in a wide straddle stance with your crotch a couple of inches above the ground.

Splits, being static stretches, should be done at the end of the workout, after you are done with all your kicking or other dynamic exercises. Isometric stretch (a type of static stretch), such as standing in the low straddle stance, are strenuous strength exercises and, like any strength exercises, are tiring—doing them before kicking will rob your kicks of their full speed, power, and stamina. Remember: tired muscles are injury prone!

The speed of progress in stretching depends on your initial levels of strength and flexibility, and on the sensibility of your total training program. Normally it takes well under a year (from a couple of months to a few months) to develop the ability to perform splits. Both the isometric stretches and standing for minutes in low stances are strength exercises, and you should apply them accordingly. Use sufficient rest between workouts. Do no more exercises than you need, and do not overwork any group of muscles.

When Things Go Wrong

Some adults have a great deal of difficulty with the side splits (but not necessarily with front splits) because of a problem in the outer part (abductors) of the hips. When the limit is reached, they feel that there is a "stop," accompanied by pain in the hip/ upper thigh region, that prevents them from opening their legs very wide.

The problem does not seem to be related to the adductors, as they do not feel much tension there. Their flexibility does improve, but at a very slow rate. Many of these individuals can perform the side split test with ease.

This is a very common problem for people who start stretching as adults. The pain and limitation of the movement sideways in the side split is caused by spreading (abducting) the thighs without tilting the pelvis forward. This tilt unwinds capsular ligaments of the hip, among them the pubofemoral ligaments, which in a normal, nonflexed position would resist excessive abduction and also push up the neck of the

femur into the cartilage collar (labrum acetabulare) at the upper edge of the hip socket.

The forward tilt of the pelvis, or hip flexion, realigns the hip joints so the ligaments relax, the neck of the femur does not jam the cartilage at the edge of the socket, and greater trochanters (bony processes on the top of the thigh bones) fit into a space behind the hip socket. This is the alignment of your hips in the proper horse stance, and this is why alignment of your hips, thighs, lower legs, and feet in a side split should be the same.

Conclusion

You need only two things to do splits with no warm-up:

- Proper alignment of your hips and thighs, which you can learn in the horse stance.
- Strong muscles of the hips and thighs, which you can develop by classical stance training (slower), or by weight lifting and isometric stretching (faster), or by using both methods for technique and strength.

This material originally appeared in the June 1997 issue of Inside Kung-Fu.

PART 4

Other Health and Training Considerations

Double Your Speed
in Thirty Days

Michael V. Abruzzi

This chapter offers you a new perspective on speed and how you can improve yours, without regard to age, rank, style, or body size. Speed is governed by your thinking, and if it is just average you are at major disadvantage as a practicing martial artist. What is the solution? Develop more speed by following the steps presented here, for an easy-to-understand path toward quicker technique. These unique exercises and training secrets are now combined to guide you toward supersonic speed skills. If you leave your preconceptions behind, there are no limits to what you can accomplish with this information.

Top students know the three types of speed and how to use them to defeat opponents in the most prestigious tournament events and precarious self-defense predicaments. Where does this leave the not-so-stellar student? Is it inevitable that these special skills and secrets remain among a small coterie of

black belts and masters? Absolutely not! Until now the only problem has been that no one has told the average student that she can be faster. Quick fighters are not born, but made through hard training. The time has arrived to reveal these speed secrets to students at every rank, from all disciplines.

Form two lines in any karate school; black belts on one side and white belts on the other. Give a command to throw a stationary backfist technique with the front hand. While the experienced display the punch with focus and speed, the performance of the lower rank student is snail-like, not targeted, and awkward. The difference is knowledge, a decision to move quickly, an understanding of body mechanics, enhanced awareness, and years of hard training. By practicing the four speed secrets and five speed exercises revealed in this text and applying the information, you will double your speed and effectiveness in thirty days or less. What does it take to be in the top ten contender brackets? How important is speed in martial arts competition today?

Hit Hard, Hit Fast, and Be First!

"Confident" best describes the defending grand champion's face. With "Terminator" emblazoned across the back of his jet black, super heavyweight uniform, he looked lean and mean—six feet two inches of muscle, protective gear, and black belt, he anxiously awaited the final battle to prove his supremacy.

Fighting his way through six grueling matches, his challenger, the overall black belt division champion of the day, moved toward the center ring with the call of his name. Standing five feet seven and one-half inches, he appeared worn down by the earlier bouts. Tired and apprehensive, he stood in the ring to face Armageddon with last year's winner. Tension shot through the crowded room like a bolt of lightning.

The long-awaited finals match for grand champion was minutes away. The air was redolent with the odor of extreme athletic competition. Because the defending champion was bigger and more experienced than the young challenger, every spectator had a theory concerning the outcome. Most of them clearly favored Terminator.

As the center judge moved the opponents into position, the crowd gathered in noisy anticipation. After a brief focusing ritual, the fighters bowed to the center official and then to each other. As the official's hand rose to mark the beginning of the competition, the onlookers grew quiet. With the signal and a yell, the match began. Adrenaline flowed like a tidal wave.

The large, defending grand champion immediately lunged forward in a straight line toward the smaller opponent. Everyone was sure Terminator would score the first point. He plowed forward like a giant steamroller preparing to flatten a fresh pile of asphalt. With a blur of movement the lighter man

shuffled to change his stance. He threw a jab to distract Terminator and connected with a point-winning left ridge hand to his headgear.

All four corner judges simultaneously yelled "Stop" after watching the lightning-fast technique connect. The movement was so quick and well executed that the center judge smiled, acknowledging the point even before the corner judges gave their decision. The smaller man used his superior speed twice again during the match, scoring a shutout victory against the reigning champion, three to zero. Frustrated, Terminator conceded. What single physical factor determined the eventual winner? Speed.

Cheetah Versus Snail

A new beauty has been added to the splendor of the world—the beauty of speed.

—Tommaso Marinetti (1876–1944)

Speed is not some phenomenon of the twentieth century, but its recognition came from our ability to gauge and rate its potential. Although unmeasurable long ago, speed has been a factor in human development since the beginning of time. Before recorded history, speed was a measure of one's ability to run away from an attacking animal without becoming its dinner. Back then, without modern instrumentation, time was a measurement of speed. A trip to town, as an example, might take three days. Today, speedometers, stopwatches, tachometers, and radar are instruments used to measure how quickly something moves.

Speed is a universal factor used to compare one thing's quickness to that of another. The more quickly something is done, the better it is considered to be, by most comparisons. A cheetah can run seventy miles per hour, while a garden snail moves only three-hundredths of a mile per hour. The cheetah is a paradigm of speed in product advertisements, while the tiny snail is absent from the copy. The fastest car wins, leaving the slowest tagged as "Grandma's grocery getter." In all worlds, from animals to automobiles, from team players to tournament competitors—faster is better.

Your Body Type

Are you endomorphic, ectomorphic, or mesomorphic? According to W. H. Sheldon's 1940 classification of body types, you are *ectomorphic* if you have a light body build, with slight muscular development. If you are *endomorphic*, you have a heavy, rounded body build, often marked by a tendency to become fat. Most Americans are this type. A *mesomorphic* person has a husky muscular build.

Dr. Sheldon's findings compared body types by their degree of roundness, softness, slenderness, fragility, muscularity, and bone development. His early definition helped to categorize people, leading to a modern version that identifies six basic body types. Each type has a proclivity toward specific athletic endeavors and martial arts styles.

1. **Short, thin-boned, small muscles.** Nearly inexhaustible, these individuals carry very little weight and have an extremely efficient metabolism. Lacking raw punching power, they make excellent flyweight fighters. Pound for pound, they are the fastest punchers in the world.

2. **Lithe, tall, small muscles.** These persons carry no more muscle mass than the thin-boned, short types, but exceed their height by nine to twelve inches. Lacking brute strength, they naturally exhibit speed and flexibility in their movements. An extra-long reach is their greatest competitive asset, making this group aesthetically pleasing in *kata* and point-sparring competition.

3. **Short, average-boned, perfect muscle dimensions.** Displaying a near-perfect ratio of strength to size, this group is agile and well balanced. Not quite as fast as their lighter counterparts, members of this group are more powerful and make excellent lightweight fighters.

4. **Low to the ground, thick-boned, massive muscles.** Nearly impossible to push off their feet, because of a low center of gravity, they exhibit great leverage and crushing power. This group does well in martial arts disciplines like *judo* and *jujitsu*, which do not require quick movements and high leg kicking maneuvers.

5. **Tall, lean, perfect muscle dimensions.** Long legs and arms enable this group to generate phenomenal speed and eye-pleasing martial arts techniques. Slightly slower because of larger muscles, this group makes the best middleweight fighters.

6. **Tall, 200-plus pounds, large muscles.** Typically slower then their leaner counterparts, this group has an impressive ratio of weight to strength, enabling them to do extremely powerful techniques. When martial artists are blessed with this body package and develop speed and balance, they are extremely hard to beat as heavyweight competitors.

Your heritage provides your genetics; your decision to be faster determines your speed. Just in case you did not pay attention in physics class, the next section explains the theory of speed.

Measurable Speed Versus Effective Speed

Speed equals distance divided by time. Measurable speed increases in two ways:

1. When distance increases with the time remaining constant
2. When time decreases

An automobile moving a distance of 60 miles in one hour is traveling at a speed of 60 miles per hour. If the distance increases to 120 miles, in a one-hour period the car is traveling at 120 miles per hour. If the same car travels 60 miles in one half-hour, the car is traveling at 120 miles per hour.

Historically, in most martial arts styles fists were held at the waist, prepared to deliver blows toward an opponent. Today, most practitioners carry their fists in a high, on-guard position near the face. Because the distance between the fist and the target is greater in the traditional style, the measurable speed of the punch is greater.

The effective force of these long-range punches is also greater when compared to the modern hands-up guarding position. A young child intuitively pulls his fist back before punching because he knows the impact will be more forceful. Moving farther from the target increases the measurable speed, but consequently increases delivery time. Simply stated, a fist closer to the target can deliver its payload first, compared to a fist held at waist level.

Rotation is the martial artist's windup before the punch. Instead of rearing back like a baseball pitcher, skilled practitioners fire off a quick twist of the body directed at the opponent. This fast, effective punching involves the legs, hips, torso, and shoulders.

> The concern is not how fast a punch travels, but how soon it arrives at its intended target.
>
> —*A master's words*

Speed is the essential factor of force. Passing the flat of your hand through the burning of a candle does not affect the flame. However, a controlled punch can extinguish the flame even stopping an inch away. Speed, not mass, is the main ingredient of effective technique.

If you double the mass of an object, you will double its impact, but if you double its speed you will quadruple its impact. Ancient warriors studied the arts to protect their lives, making effective force the ultimate factor. Today's martial artists are sports ori-

ented, and the winner connects first. Want to be faster? If so, learn the three types of speed to develop a quicker delivery.

The Three Types of Speed

Total speed is a synergistic combination of perception, reaction, and action. A complete understanding of all three facets is necessary to double your fighting speed in thirty days. Each explanation includes exercise and speed secrets to enhance understanding and hasten your results.

Perceptual Speed

Perceptual speed is the quickness of senses, with hearing and sight the prime considerations. Maintaining alertness increases this type of speed. To create quick reflex action, hear without listening. A blind person learns to use his ears to react to noise. Martial artists train to become more aware by blocking out all that is unimportant. This single-minded focus decreases a fighter's response time. Allowing nothing to create a distraction is the first key to heightened awareness.

The second is seeing quickly, allowing you to dominate the faster, larger opponent, whatever your level of experience. Whether the situation is athletic or life and death, if you see quickly, you will become almost invincible.

Learning to explode in that critical instant between your opponent's decision to act and the start of her motion catches her completely off-guard. You can neutralize even unfamiliar techniques and speed up counterattacks to an adversary. Your opponent's fastest moves will seem to crawl when you learn to look without seeing. *Soft eye* is the first of the four speed secrets revealed here to guarantee you faster reflexes.

Speed Secret 1: Soft Eye

Straight, erect posture creates good vision and focus. Look directly over your opponent's shoulders. Continue to stare past his body at any fixed object. This unique visual state is *soft eye*. The background will become almost blurred. Your opponent's image will seem to project toward you. He will be the only thing you see clearly, allowing you to act or react quickly. This full body viewing allows you to detect the intentions of your opponent, from head to toe, in one glance.

Implementation of this procedure is a matter of intent. Use it whenever you choose; there is no adverse effect to your eyesight.

Two exercises can help you quickly increase your eye speed and strength for enhanced perception.

Speed Exercise 1: Pencil Pushups

Some people's eyes do not converge properly when they're doing close work. To see if that is a problem for you, hold a pencil at arm's length. Start moving it toward your eyes. Stop when you see two pencils. If your hand is about seven inches from your face, then you have convergence insufficiency.

To correct the problem, do the exercise again. This time, attempt to see just one pencil. Move the pencil closer, then away. Keep trying to focus as the pencil moves in and out. Within a week of practicing this for five minutes each day, you will develop the ability to view a single pencil from a position two inches from your eye. Fast reaction starts with your ability to see the incoming technique clearly. This exercise will help you make this determination even when the punches and kicks are close to your face.

Speed Exercise 2: Eye Sprinting

Place a magazine about ten feet away from where you are standing. Next, hold another magazine at your normal reading distance, usually about twelve to fourteen inches away from your nose. Train your eyes on the closest magazine. Now look at the periodical ten feet away. Refocus your eyes as they jump from magazine to magazine.

Do this for five minutes a day and you will develop the ability to focus more quickly on objects far and near. Practicing allows you to detect incoming movements from your opponent more clearly.

Reactive Speed

Reactive speed is the quickness of the mind to select appropriate movements to effectively deal with incoming kicks and punches. Action and reaction are not equal. This simple statement explains why you can strike someone without being blocked. Conversely, this allows people to hit you before you can defend yourself. This form of speed is the easiest to develop because it responds to someone's offensive intentions.

Reaction time, breath control, and concentration are factors that define an increase in your reactive speed. These factors must be coordinated to attain maximum efficiency. The best method to achieve a decrease in your reaction time is to work with a partner delivering a variety of techniques toward you. Practice by blocking and moving to parry her offensive maneuvers. Exhale during the execution of each defensive counter. Focus and single-minded concentration are only apparent when you exhale. Practice breathing slowly and deeply when you feel anxious. Visualize yourself as a pond, beautiful, blue, and calm, waiting to react with a powerful splash when a diver enters your water. Practice can be fun. Try this interaction with a willing partner to increase your speed in no time.

Speed Exercise 3: Paper Chase

Tear a piece of paper into small squares. Have a partner hold them at your shoulder height. Reach out to grab the bits of paper as your partner tries to pull them away, challenging your ability to catch one. Continue to practice this until you can grab most of the papers before your partner can move them out of reach.

Speed Exercise 4: Blow for Blow

Target practice using sound as a stimulus is a great way to increase your speed. Have a training partner hold a target bag. With a whistle in his mouth he can blow to indicate a time for you to strike the bag. With each sound, try to hit the bag as quickly as you can. Challenge yourself; continue the exercise at an ever-increasing pace, varying the strikes and kicks. Have your training partner move around the floor to increase the challenge. Compare your reaction times as the exercise continues. You will notice your response times decreasing as you practice.

Speed Exercise 5: Is Anybody Out There?

Shadowboxing is a great method for building speed. Picture an opponent standing in front of you and trying to hit you. Use your imagination and try to anticipate the moves of your invisible adversary. Stamina and endurance build in this practice, allowing you to keep your speed consistent throughout an actual match. By practicing without fear of injury, you can experiment with fast defensive and offensive moves against your invisible opponent.

Active Speed

Active speed is the quickness of the body to move when the mind decides to attack. Barring neurological impairment, everyone is capable of lightning-fast performance. The current speed of your movement is habitual and reinforced during your formative years, ages one through four. If you grew up hearing, "You're lazy and slow," this has likely become a lifestyle for you. Quickness of physical motion begins in the mind as a visualization of yourself. This mind-view expresses itself in the actual movement.

The force of a punch starts at the toes as they push down to the floor, then travels through the knee to the twisted hip. The power line continues to travel through the rotating torso, shoulders, forearm, wrist, and finally the knuckle.

Actual speed is a combination of accumulated body movement; taken in the proper order, your speed will increase automatically. By visualizing and producing this motion in order, you will not have

conflicting movement, slowing your punch. Introduce the linked movement as late as possible at each level to take full advantage of the peak speed of each body part.

Speed Secret 2: See Spot Run . . . Fast!

Concentrate on a spot on your forearm just below the wrist before you punch. Begin your punch by physically pressing your toes into the floor. Continue the force line through your knee, torso, and shoulder. Focus all your thought on the forearm point. Visualize this spot projecting forward toward your target with supersonic speed when the combined body movement reaches the forearm, like a rocket booster. When you concentrate on this small point and its rapid movement, your fist will seem to fly through the space at your opponent. To increase your kicking speed, visualize an analogous point on your ankle.

Think about what happens when you turn on a garden hose. Water immediately begins to come out the end slowly, even if the water from the faucet just started. Water at the end of the hose "knows" that you have opened the faucet long before new water from the faucet arrives at the end.

Everything accelerates gradually. Take advantage of the speed and force generated by the total body movement before moving the fist. Like a bullet fired from a gun, your punch can move quickly if you concentrate on an extremely large energy burst to initiate each part of the technique. Because of the powerful force that propels it forward, a bullet goes from zero to maximum velocity in approximately one-tenth of a second.

Tension and unnecessary muscular contractions act as brakes, reducing speed and dissipating energy. One obstacle the novice athlete must overcome in competition is the natural tendency to try too hard. Tyros often attempt to blast every possible technique at once. An athlete does best when she simply lets go, rather than trying too hard. If you are running as fast as you can, do not feel as though you should be running faster.

Speed Secret 3: Learn to Squeeze

Another key to speed is in the lower body. In a ready stance, tuck your hips and bend your knees slightly. To develop forward speed, tighten your buttocks by squeezing. This moves your hips forward, and you will feel as if someone is pushing you from behind.

Try this movement, keeping your back and head straight—the sensation is amazing. This secret is good for use in free sparring and *kata*. Beginners often find that their best lunges never can overtake a senior student, yet the experienced practitioner can overcome the beginner at the end of his lunge. A senior relies on his speed, generated by flexing the buttocks, to land his attack, closing the gap in less time. This method allows one to close the attacking distance more quickly and gives greater initial speed to any technique.

Six Ways to Develop More Active Speed

1. **Relax before striking.** Relax your muscles until you are three inches from the target. Tense up at the last moment to achieve maximum force and quickness. Stay as loose as possible; tension reduces speed.

2. **Increase flexibility.** Your ability to stretch does more than produce impressive kicks; it is necessary to increase speed.

3. **Use movements that follow direct angles and paths.** Work toward economy of motion, as the shortest distance between two points is a straight line. Avoid erroneous angles and strike with the closest weapon through the shortest distance.

4. **Mobility and spring are necessary components of fast technique.** An object that is moving will continue to move until acted upon by another object. It is more difficult to push an automobile from a standing position than it is to push one already rolling.

5. **Build a resistance to fatigue.** Stamina and endurance training are important when you are attempting to increase your fighting speed. A tired fighter is always slow.

6. **Snap out equals snap back.** Have you ever snapped someone with a towel? Then you already know that to have any zing to an attack you have to pull back as hard as you push out.

Many fighters fail to understand that quickness depends on many factors; practicing basic skills is essential. Where you stand compared with your opponent is another important aspect of increasing your effective speed.

Your Stasis Position

Every karate style has its ready stance. Few practitioners understand that this seemingly innocuous basic position is a key to speed in defensive and offensive movement. Distance has to do with your physical position and its relationship to your opponent. The closer you are to your opponent, the more quickly you can deliver a punch. The opponent's reach will determine your safe standing distance. Remember, keep it close to keep it fast.

To Be Hard or to Be First?

What do you want to accomplish? Traditional strikes and kicks deliver powerful focused results. Speed techniques arrive at the target point first. All karate techniques are either *linear* (straight-lined) or *arced* (curved) in their release. Decreasing the distance between you and your opponent increases the effective speed of both deliveries.

The speed of arced technique has one additional advantage: if you shorten the radius of the arc, you increase the speed. A baseball batter can push backward on his front leg just before the impact point to the ball, decreasing the arc and thus increasing speed. In the same way, martial artists can push back just before the point of contact to increase speed.

Traditional technique and speed technique are terms used to differentiate the moves in this section. Comparing each allows you to judge which will provide your desired outcome. In every illustration pushing back on the front leg at the last minute will increase the speed of the strike.

Roundhouse Kick

A traditional roundhouse kick draws the knee to the body with a vertical angle. The foot then moves in an arc from the high raised knee forward to the desired target. This produces a powerful kick directed at the area of your choice.

A speed roundhouse kick works with the knowledge that the shortest distance between two points is a straight line. When executing it, chamber the knee toward the body only enough to allow proper execution of the technique. The fastest kick is the one that travels the shortest radius from the hip. Keep your foot close to your opponent. Push back at the last instant with the support leg to increase the speed.

Front Snap Kick

A traditional front snap kick draws the knee to the body with a vertical angle. The foot then moves from the high raised knee in a vertical arc toward the desired target. A speed front snap kick raises the knee only as high as necessary, allowing a fast delivery through a shortened radius.

Knife-Hand Strike

A traditional knife-hand attack can assume a horizontal or vertical radius by maintaining the elbow position close to the body. For speed, hold the hand as close to the opponent's body as possible, with the technique firing out through the shortest radius.

Hammer Fist

A traditional hammer fist attack can assume a horizontal or vertical radius by maintaining the elbow position close to the body. For speed, hold the hand as close to the opponent's body as possible, with the technique firing out through the shortest radius. Make your choice of hard or fast, execute the technique, and savor the results.

Can the Food You Eat Affect Your Speed?

Yes, you are what you eat. Carbohydrates give the body fuel to generate energy for kicks and punches. That candy bar or any simple carbohydrate you eat before class will cause you to feel a quick energy boost. Your body reacts by releasing to the brain serotonin, a neurotransmitter that plays a key role in your mood. As the makers of antidepressant medications have so profitably discovered, tinkering with the levels of serotonin alters a person's sense of well-being and energy. However, when the sugar buzz is gone, you are drowsier than Grandpa after Thanksgiving dinner.

Complex carbohydrates such as whole wheat bread, grains, and vegetables metabolize in your body slowly and are a good source of energy before competition. They will keep your blood sugar levels stable over a longer time, providing you with a steadier energy supply from your food. Properly fueled muscles produce fast action and reaction techniques as needed.

Speed Secret 4: Take Two, and See Me in the Morning

The lack of vitamin B_{12} will cause a degree of slowness in your technique. Test yourself for possible deficiency of this important body building block. Lie on your back, drawing your knees to your chest. Have someone push against your knee from the front; resist as he pushes. Next, have your partner extend your leg fully and return it to the bent position. Try to resist again after the stretch as your partner pushes.

If you are unable to resist the movement, you are deficient in vitamin B_{12}. Eliminate this problem by taking a supplement with your complete breakfast every day. Consult a physician for the recommended dosage.

It's All Up to You!

Journey to that special place that few have visited—the winner's circle, a dream for many and a reality for some. The speed secrets and breakthrough exercises described here provide the physical path. This information shows you what you can accomplish. Isn't it time for you to be consistently triumphant?

> When the time is right, even a mouse can become a tiger.
>
> —*Japanese maxim*

This material originally appeared in the August 1998 issue of Inside Karate.

The Physical Profile
of Elite Kickboxers

Christopher Hess

Fifth-degree *Tae Kwon Do* black belt and professional kickboxer Chuck Wolfe read the "findings" with a smile. A Canadian research study entitled "Physiological and Anthropometric Profile of Elite Kickboxers" conclusively proved that elite kickboxers are the best among all athletes, not just other kickboxers.

This is no big surprise to Wolfe, who wonders why the recognition is so long in coming. Since beginning his kickboxing career in 1987, Wolfe has compiled an impressive 39-4-1 record with 21 knockouts. He was also the world light heavyweight champion (K.I.C.K.) for nearly two years and has been the U.S. champion since April of 1995.

In this chapter, we'll look at how the training and success of a champion like Wolfe reflects the findings of that Canadian study, which can be found in the *Journal of Strength and Conditioning Research*, volume 9, issue 4, pages 240–42.

Finding 1: High Aerobic Capacity

The research conducted with elite male kickboxers revealed high aerobic capacity among them. Aerobic activity, from the layman's perspective, is generally understood as the ability to perform extended exercise at moderate intensity (usually 65 to 85 percent of maximum heart rate) for more than twenty minutes.

In controlled laboratory measurements, elite kickboxers had recorded values of aerobic capacity that are comparable to a person who runs a 4:45 mile, or a 34-minute 10K foot race. If you haven't been to the track or a local 10K recently, that's fast! This doesn't mean all elite kickboxers could necessarily run at those speeds (without specific training), but their aerobic values are the same as those who do.

After twenty-three years of martial arts training and recently turning forty years old, Chuck Wolfe is committed to aerobic training as an essential foundation of his success. He runs four days per week, usually covering five miles in thirty-six minutes.

To gauge his progress, he performs a "twelve-minute test" every eight weeks, running as many laps as possible around a quarter-mile track in twelve minutes. The results give him an approximate value of his aerobic capacity and also help him gauge his recovery ability. To find out whether you have elite-level aerobic capacity, try running as many laps as you can in twelve minutes. Based on the number of laps run, you will have the corresponding (approximate) values:

Distance (miles)	Laps	Aerobic capacity
1.0	4	25
1.25	5	33
1.5	6	42
1.75	7	51
2.0	8	60

To have characteristics similar to elite kickboxers, you would need to run slightly over eight laps in your test, because their average aerobic capacity is approximately 62. The advantage to this test is that it is accessible to everyone and only costs twelve minutes of time. The disadvantage is that it is not as precise as laboratory assessments and will take some number crunching to determine values that do not represent complete laps.

On a final note, by taking his heart rate at the end of all his runs, Wolfe also knows whether he is over- or undertraining and adjusts his training accordingly.

Finding 2: High Anaerobic Capacity

The research study also noted high anaerobic capacity. Anaerobic activity is characterized by short, intense efforts performed in the absence of molecular oxygen, usually up to six seconds in length (as in a sprint or flurry of punches). The study demonstrates that elite kickboxers have higher values than elite American wrestlers. In fact, the recorded values place elite kickboxers above the 95th percentile of the entire male population!

Wolfe employs a sophisticated, science-based approach to anaerobic training developed in part by coach David Cannada, who teaches boxing at the Quivira Sports and Health Club of Overland Park, Kansas. In conjunction with a Cleveland-based company called Performance Concepts, Inc., Cannady developed the PunchMaster, which is a regular feature of Wolfe's anaerobic workouts. This device was also used in training for the 1992 Olympics.

The PunchMaster features sensors in a water-filled punching bag that are connected to a computer and displayed on a TV screen. The screen displays the number of punches thrown per minute and how much time remains in a round. Wolfe specifies the number of punches desired in a round, and the PunchMaster warns him if he exceeds or falls below the desired training intensity. At the end of the round (or the entire workout), the PunchMaster provides instant feedback with a recap of the workout.

To integrate some of his aerobic and anaerobic training needs in the same workout, Wolfe also uses the "forty-two step" method in his running workouts. He begins his sessions by walking, and then on the forty-second step begins jogging. After forty-two more steps, he sprints, after forty-two strides at the sprint intensity, he walks again. By practicing this walk-run-sprint-walk cycle, he stimulates three important capacities for a kickboxer: aerobic, anaerobic, and recovery.

Finding 3: Knee Torque

One laboratory test measured the magnitude of force generated by the knee at various joint angles to demonstrate knee extension peak torque. The test subjects' results were similar to elite Alpine skiers and only slightly lower than elite sprinters and jumpers.

To train properly for his matches, Wolfe uses both plyometric and resistance training that strengthens his knee torque and, ultimately, his ability to throw fast, powerful kicks. For the lower body, he uses the quadriceps extension, leg press, and calf raises. He doesn't use squats in his routine because that exercise has caused him problems in his hamstrings.

Approximately eight weeks before a match, Wolfe focuses on strength training for about six weeks and then tapers off to rest and incorporate the gains from intense training. For the upper body, he uses the seated row, dumbbells (on the incline bench), and exercises for the latissimus dorsi.

Finding 4: Low Body Fat

At a mean weight of 160 pounds, the average body-fat percentage among the elite kickboxers was 8.1, which is similar to that found in elite male endurance athletes. This quantity is substantially lower than the 12- to 15-percent average among elite boxers.

At six feet two inches and 174 pounds, Wolfe's body-fat percentage is consistent with the characteristics of elite kickboxers. His secret? He avoids fried foods and has a very low-fat, high-carbohydrate diet. He only eats meat one time per week and believes in separating nutrients—that is, he eats protein sources separate from carbohydrate sources. He tries to avoid mixing the two, which he believes retards digestion.

Implications

After reviewing the Canadian study and some of Wolfe's training methods, you might wonder if they would work for you. Just ask Doug Freeman, who trains under Wolfe and is currently ranked fourth in the world (K.I.C.K.) in the super welterweight division. Freeman uses the same running program, PunchMaster drills, and plyometric training.

In summary, the physical profile of an elite kickboxer includes high capacities of the aerobic and anaerobic energy systems along with tremendous knee torque and low body fat.

Christopher Hess is a Specialist in Martial Art Conditioning (SMAC). This material originally appeared in the January 1997 issue of Inside Karate.

11

Fitness Through Boxing

Robert Ferguson

You train hard six times per week, blasting your muscles with weights and honing your skills in the *dojo* (training hall). Despite your intensity, do you feel your martial arts training is missing something? If so, consider fitness through boxing and its focus mitt training.

Combining cardiovascular, anaerobic, coordination, speed, and focus training, boxing's mitt training gives you a total-body workout that will certainly enhance your martial arts skills. To benefit from this workout, you need discipline, dedication, desire, thirty minutes per day, and, most important, a partner. In time, it may prove to become an essential and preferred method for you to maintain your overall fitness. You will also improve mentally and strategically as a self-defense practitioner.

Focus mitt training will add an invaluable edge to your current training program. By simply incorporating the science of boxing into your daily practices, you will make a quantum leap toward becoming combat effective. Boxing's focus mitt training teaches and develops definitive self-defense attributes such as slipping, bobbing and weaving, and its four strikes: *jab*, *cross*, *hook*, and *uppercut*.

Although the science of boxing has proven on many occasions to be effective for street fighting, the same does not go for the traditional chambered punches. The traditional chambered punch is presented in the classroom as a practical technique, yet it has proven to be detrimental in street fights. Why, you may ask? The answer is quite simple, especially when you are faced with a seasoned street fighter who is familiar with slap boxing, street wrestling, and ungarnished bare-knuckle fistfighting. When the traditional martial artist performs a strike such as a reverse punch and one hand is chambered on his waist, he is obviously exposed for a seasoned fighter to capitalize on the opening.

If a martial artist comes into conflict with a street fighter, that fighter is likely well equipped with boxing skills. In America, boxing is a mainstream approach to street fighting. Even in our prisons, criminals practice boxing, not *kata*. Many fathers teach their sons how to box. Therefore, to be able to defend a boxer's attack you must first be able to fight like a boxer. Focus mitt training will enhance your self-defense skills and understanding of what makes boxing effective.

While training within the framework of boxing, don't discard your traditional way of properly making a fist and striking soft tissue areas of the body. The science of boxing alone makes you merely a boxer; with traditional training in striking without a glove and hand wraps on, you become a skilled fighter.

Case in point: it was reported that Mike Tyson broke his hand in a street fight with former heavyweight contender Mitch Green, and Muhammad Ali broke his hand three times in the ring while wearing gloves. They both sustained these injuries because of their lack of training without hand wraps, tape, and gloves. Neither of these highly skilled boxers trained to strike with their bare hands.

Boxing will enhance your fighting abilities, and traditional training will ensure that you develop a strong, straight wrist, tight fist, and innate ability to vary striking force for specific parts of the body. Fitness through boxing utilizing the focus mitts will get you in better shape and complement your traditional martial arts training.

Common Concerns

Let's look at some of the most common concerns expressed about focus mitt training.

Focus Mitt Holder

The person holding the mitt benefits as much as the person striking does. One must be focused and knowledgeable of the various strikes in order to properly position and hold the focus mitts. In addition, the person holding the mitt must provide a little resistance when the partner strikes. The holder will obviously get an awesome workout while learning the science of boxing.

Improper Technique

Jab, cross, hook, and uppercut must be delivered correctly. In boxing, it is the body, not the arms, that makes the techniques effective. In the uppercut, the legs make the strike powerful. The same goes for the jab, cross, and hook. For instance, while executing a hook you don't simply swing your arm wildly. Instead, you position your arm in an L shape and pivot on the ball of the foot relative to the hand performing the hook.

Dropping Guard

If you practice a martial art that teaches forms (*kata*), you may find yourself chambering the hand on the hip, which leaves you open. If you execute a jab, be sure your opposite hand rests alongside your cheek. The same goes for performing a hook, uppercut, and cross. The opposite hand covers the open side. Be careful not to drop your guard when executing a strike, or you will be open for a counterstrike.

Developing Rhythm

If you strike more than once in sequence, it is considered a *combination*. For instance, jab, cross, and hook alternating arms is a three-count combination. Keep in mind, you should strike one at a time, yet load up on your last strike and maintain good technique.

Body Movement

Body movement and stepping are important components of the science of boxing. Many martial arts schools emphasize blocking first and striking second. But in boxing you hear words like *bob*, *weave*, *slip*, and *side step*. As I have always advocated, if you have time to block, you have time to counter or move out of the way.

Bill "Superfoot" Wallace advocates the same thing. He states, "If I can get you to block, I can create an opening." Learning to use your body more effectively is an attribute developed after becoming proficient with the science of boxing and its focus mitt drills. Your partner will prove to be critical in your honing the skills that result from boxing practice.

With activities such as cardioboxing being promoted in martial arts schools and fitness centers around the world, it is clear that fitness through boxing is going to bridge the gap between the self-defense and fitness industries.

Robert Ferguson is a California-based freelance writer and co-author of A Guide to Rape Awareness and Prevention and Self-Defense for Today's Woman. *Ferguson is the co-owner of Elite Training Center, located in Agoura Hills, California, and founder of Cardio Self-Defense. This material originally appeared in the October 1997 issue of* Inside Karate.

Abdominal Training
for the Martial Artist

Norm Leff

The most overlooked muscles of the body are the abdominal muscles. The midsection is composed of the rectus abdominis (pulls the trunk forward), external oblique (bends the trunk to the side and rotates the trunk), and the internal oblique, which assists the external oblique.

All the abdominal exercises affect the lower-back area (erector spinae). In other words, the midsection consists of the front abdominal muscles and the muscles of the lower back and sides.

Most bodybuilders and weight trainers concentrate on developing the muscles of the arms, chest, shoulders, back, and legs. Often, the abdominal muscles are completely neglected.

If you visit the Tate Gallery and the National Gallery in London, you will see statues of Greek mythological figures such as Apollo and Hercules. The one section of these bodies that will immediately catch your attention is the perfect abdominals. In particular, the sides of the waist (oblique muscles) were emphasized.

The midsection is the link between the upper and lower body. A muscular and trim midsection will enhance one's physical appearance, and is an indication of physical fitness.

Many physical fitness instructors consider the abdominal region the center of health. They believe the development of the midsection will improve one's health and vitality. It is also a simple way to relieve constipation.

Antonio Rocca, who was one of the most popular wrestlers some years ago, believed that the center of movement and energy for every sport and physical activity is the twisting and turning ability of the waist. Rocca said: "Observe a good wrestler, boxer, martial artist, golfer, tennis player, baseball player, soccer player, etc. Every blow, every swing, every throw, and every forceful movement starts not with the arms or shoulders, but with the twist of the waist." That is why the mark of every athlete in good condition is a trim, hard, muscular waistline.

Abdominal training should play a very important part in your training program. A former U.S. Olympic weight-lifting coach stated that all weight lifters he had trained had to practice abdominal movements that bend, twist, exercise, and activate the abdominal section. For this type of exercise improves every internal process, including the digestive system, assimilation, elimination, and glandular action; in addition, it builds strength and lifting ability. It also improves health and power. He felt that all of us need plenty of abdominal exercise.

Other famous and well-known physical fitness gurus feel that having a trim and muscular midsection gives one better health; more energy, pep, vitality, and stamina; and a more attractive body. Former strongman and physical fitness teacher Vic Boff said: "A fat-encumbered body is a hindrance to longevity." He also teaches that the waistline is the lifeline, and that every inch added to the abdomen after the age of forty takes off one year of life. Boff adds that abdominal exercises can help eliminate constipation, and protect against hernia (rupture) and visceral prolapse (sagging of the abdominal region).

Exercising the midsection is for everyone. All of us will receive health benefits from abdominal training. Bear in mind that a weak abdominal region contributes to lower-back problems, which become chronic with time.

All grappling instructors will tell you that grapplers need strong abdominal and waist muscles for grappling. Whether you are a freestyle wrestler, Greco-Roman wrestler, pro wrestler, *judo* grappler, *jujitsu* grappler, or *sambo* wrestler, you need to have a well-conditioned and powerful midsection.

If you are into the striking, kicking, and boxing arts, the same advice applies to you. Punching, thrusting, kicking, blocking, turning, dodging, evading, and other important skills require a powerful midsection.

Antonio Rocca and Andre Drapp were both outstanding professional wrestlers and athletes. Both had exceptional physiques, and abdominal exercises played a very important part in their training routines. Drapp was a Mr. France and a Mr. Europe and had the abdominal development of a Greek statue. Rocca was an Italian Hercules with a Herculean body. These athletes were my idols and heroes, and my inspiration for developing my physique. I considered them men of great size and strength.

Fitness guru Jack LaLanne is a great believer in abdominal exercises. His success as a physical fitness teacher and nutrition advisor is rooted in his basic philosophy on exercise:

1. Establish a goal.
2. Get into the habit of exercising every day.
3. Do the exercises in sets.
4. Do a little more each day than you did the day before.
5. Make a supreme effort to concentrate while exercising. The more you concentrate on the muscles being worked, the sooner you'll see results.
6. Self-resistance makes the exercise more effective.
7. Train, don't strain. Don't overdo any of the exercises. Crawl, then walk, then run.
8. Don't give up and quit! Many people give up because exercising is difficult.
9. Strengthen your willpower!
10. Eat nutritious food. Avoid eating junk food such as candy, cake, ice cream, pizza, and fried foods.
11. Achieving your goal is a matter of self-interest.
12. The secret of life is that it's not so much what you have that counts, but what you do with what you have.

When Jack was in his fifties he would get up every morning at 4:00 A.M. and exercise for two hours or more.

Train your abdominal muscles six days per week for at least twenty or thirty minutes per session. If you want to train them longer, you may. Or, you can train your abdominal and waist muscles ten minutes in the morning, ten minutes in the afternoon, and then ten minutes at night. I train my abs forty to sixty minutes, six times per week. Sometimes I train them twice a day. Your training schedule will depend on your interest, need, and time. Whatever you do, be consistent. Have a goal in mind and accomplish it. Consistency is the key to success. Begin slowly, and increase the workload and intensity of the exercises as you get stronger.

This material originally appeared in the January 1999 issue of Inside Karate.

Neglecting the Basics

Joseph J. Estwanik, M.D.

A competitor needs more than good intentions. Fitness represents an integral facet of the martial arts. Yet many fail to pay the price to be valid participants in a competition. Let me provide some very recent examples that emphasize this.

Last month I served as ringside physician for two professional events. On Saturday night, I covered a so-called "pro boxing" show and performed the very important prebout physicals as well as the normal ringside duties. While performing the physicals, I always find it quite useful and revealing to ask athletes how many miles they run per week. This gives me a reasonable handle on their level of fitness, their dedication, and their professionalism. Their "miles-per-week" is scribbled on the bout sheet as a personal guide when I supervise the upcoming bout. Prior experience (number of amateur bouts and number of pro bouts) is also transcribed next to the name. This usually enables me to predict problems, mismatches, and even outcomes.

I am sure that you already know my conclusions. Those who didn't pay their dues for fitness were the consistent losers. Five out of six bouts that night were won by technical knockout. One dominant winner was a former marine with 150 amateur bouts who exemplified physical fitness. No serious injuries occurred; however, several disgracefully ill-prepared athletes took a beating because they were too tired to protect themselves and to sustain an offense. A bout can be honorably lost if one is outscored by a skilled opponent. Conversely, it can be embarrassingly lost, before one even steps into the ring, by neglected fitness. Most important, fitness equals safety, and a lack of fitness equals a lack of safety.

Thursday night, I examined fourteen pro kickboxers, including two novice women. Most bouts were scheduled for only three rounds of two minutes. As usual, the competitors were questioned about training levels. Both were evenly matched by weight, and it was only the second competition for each. When I asked one woman about her level of running, she knowingly informed me that "Running is not healthy for women." This ill-prepared, health-conscious competitor didn't seem to understand that she was about to step through the ropes into a very serious full-contact event. What do you think happened? I am sure you correctly guessed again! I was forced to stop her fight at the end of the second round as she stood defenseless in the corner, covering up and taking blow after blow because she was completely fatigued.

Trained martial artists are to be congratulated on their preparation and dedication to fitness. They set standards for training. Many so-called "pro boxers" can't hold a candle to the fitness level of properly prepared martial artists. During my many years of ringside duties for such events as the Ultimate Fighting Championship and Battlecade Extreme Fighting, I witnessed many fine examples of proper preparedness and dedicated physical training—true professionalism in the fitness arena!

Running isn't the only method for achieving cardiovascular fitness, of course. Just as one can rarely win with one punch, instead of practiced combinations, one can rarely achieve overall fitness with just one type of exercise. A variety of punching drills, short sprints, interval boxing, bicycling, jump rope, swimming, kicking sequences, and other techniques are all viable options. Overuse injuries can be greatly reduced by diversity in your workouts. However, don't forget your strength training and stretching. Keep up the good work, and I'll see you in the ring!

This material originally appeared in the April 1999 issue of Martial Arts Illustrated.

Biomechanics— for a Lifetime of Mobility

Christine Lydon, M.D.

There are three basic joint types: *fibrous* (like the sutures of the skull); *cartilaginous* (like the vertebrae and intervertebral discs); and *synovial*, which allow for free movement (as in the wrist, elbow, knees, and fingers) Synovial joints incorporate a fluid-filled space lined by a layer of tissue known as the *synovial membrane*. Muscles, tendons, ligaments and cartilage surround, connect, and lend stability to the bones that comprise the joint. Injury to any of these structures may lead to pain, degenerative changes, and decreased range of motion. A basic understanding of musculoskeletal biomechanics will help you to decrease your risk of injury and maximize the effectiveness of your workouts.

The Fundamentals of Biomechanics

Biomechanics is the study of the material properties of biological materials. With virtually no exception, every tissue in the human body possesses viscoelastic material properties. When a deforming force is applied to a viscoelastic material, it will flow like a fluid (viscosity) and stretch like a spring (elasticity). Silly Putty is a perfect example of a viscoelastic material. Simply stated, bones, ligaments, muscles, tendons, and cartilage all behave like Silly Putty when subjected to tensile forces.

If you pulled a piece of Silly Putty slowly, it would stretch or "flow" for some distance without breaking as long as you continued to apply a steady tensile force. On the other hand, if you were to take this same piece of Silly Putty and yank on it, it would likely snap before stretching too far. The more rapidly you try to stretch the Silly Putty, the stiffer it gets, the more force you must apply, and the more easily it snaps. Hence, the rate of force application has a measurable effect on viscosity. Now let's stick the Silly Putty in the refrigerator for a while. When we take it out and try to pull it, we have a hard time getting it to stretch or "flow." The colder the Silly Putty, the stiffer it becomes, the more it resists tensile forces, and the more easily it snaps. Hence, temperature also has a measurable effect on viscosity.

Elasticity permits a material to recoil back to its original length after it's been stretched. For example, say you took a spring and stretched it to a new length. Within a defined range of length changes, the spring returns to its original length after the deforming force is removed. If you were to take this same spring and extend it beyond a certain limit, the spring would sustain irreversible damage and no longer recoil fully once the force is removed.

The basic material properties we have outlined have countless applications in the world of athletics.

The Importance of Warming Up

Rule number one: never tax a cold muscle. Remember what happened when the Silly Putty was refrigerated? Our muscles, tendons, and ligaments react in a similar manner. A "cold" muscle feels stiff and weak, and, relative to a warm muscle, *is* stiff and weak. Similarly, a warm tendon will accommodate more stretch prior to injury than a cold tendon. A cold ligament is far less likely to "flow" with the force.

Before participating in any athletic activity, including stretching, drills, or weight training, you should raise your peripheral body temperature. Get your heart beating and increase the bloodflow to your extremities by participating in five minutes of low-intensity cardiovascular activity. Try doing slow pushups or jumping jacks if you are on the field or in the *dojo*. Hop on the stationary bike or treadmill if you're at the gym.

Proper Stretching Techniques

Volumes have been written on the importance of stretching to promote strength and flexibility, and martial artists are certainly among the most devoted stretchers. Unfortunately, ignorance of basic musculoskeletal biomechanics precludes the modification of some archaic practices that involve dangerous stretching techniques. Moreover, even the most ardent stretchers tend to neglect this aspect of their routine when it comes to weight lifting. Despite overwhelming evidence supporting its benefits, far too many athletes fail to make stretching part of their strength-training regimen.

By reducing muscle tension and promoting relaxation, stretching enhances the quality of recovery time, the period when muscle growth occurs. In theory, stretching loosens the fascial envelopes that form muscle compartments. This may lead to improved circulation and freer muscular development. In addition, consistent stretching helps prevent injuries by allowing for freer, more integrated movements. The increased body awareness that accompanies stretching makes it easier for the athlete to target a specific muscle or muscle group during an exercise. Believe it or not, regular stretching actually improves both strength and coordination. However, it is not enough to simply stretch. A basic knowledge of human physiology and tissue biomechanics can provide the athlete with all the tools necessary for proper stretching.

Stretching can be done with or without the aid of a partner. If you move your body into a stretched position, you are engaged in *active stretching*. In *passive stretching*, a partner provides the force to move into and hold the stretch. The two most basic stretching styles are referred to as *static stretching* and *ballistic stretching*. Static stretching involves moving slowly into a stretched position and holding that position for a desired period. This technique is simple to perform and safe for your joints. Ballistic stretching calls for sharp, rapid movements and uses the body's momentum to theoretically augment the range of stretch. Going back to our Silly Putty analogy, human tissue resists force when it is applied rapidly. Tendons and ligaments tighten when they are stretched too quickly. Tendons and ligaments that are stretched rapidly will sustain injury compared to the same tendons and ligaments stretched gradually. Moreover, protective reflex arc causes muscles to contract when tendons sense a rapid length change. Muscles will also contract in response to pain. It is obviously impossible to achieve a full stretch with contracted muscles! The message is simple: Always stretch gradually to a point of mild discomfort, not outright pain. Never bounce. Instead, hold the stretched position for about twenty seconds.

Don't limit yourself to a preworkout stretch. Continue to stretch frequently during your workout to promote circulation. It is especially important to stretch after your workout, when lactic acid levels are at a maximum and your muscles are hungry for glycogen replenishment. By increasing bloodflow to a muscle, waste products like lactic acid are rapidly removed to help prevent muscle soreness. In addition, more blood-borne nutrients are available for energy and growth.

There are countless different stretches designed to include the basic muscle groups. A detailed description of these techniques goes beyond the scope of this chapter. However, by following the general guidelines given here, you can be assured that your stretching program will reap maximum benefits with little risk of injury.

Proper Weight-Training Techniques

Weight training is an art that cannot be mastered overnight. I have seen world-class athletes walk into a gym and throw weights around with about as much finesse (and effectiveness) as a chimpanzee. For every correct way to perform an exercise, there are a dozen ways to do it wrong. Improper training techniques inevitably lead to injury, wasted hours, and an asymmetric physique. We all know people who spend their life in the gym and never seem to make any progress. And who isn't familiar with the martini-glass syndrome? Big chest, big arms, flat butt, and pencil legs. The typical martini glass does lots of arm curls and bench presses. He believes that they are the manliest exercises and they're all one really needs anyway. Usually his form is so poor that no matter what body part he attempts to work, he cheats with his chest and biceps. The imbalance between well-developed pecs and underdeveloped lats will eventually lead to a hunched posture, and the late stages of martini-glass syndrome can resemble a humpback.

When learning to train with weights, movements must be slow and steady with strict attention to form. I suggest holding the full contraction for a short pause to accentuate the pump. Concentrate on both the concentric and eccentric phases of the contraction to maximize every repetition. Learn what using specific muscle groups "feels like" and duplicate this feeling when trying new exercises for the same body part.

Most important, avoid sharp, jerky repetitions and using momentum to lift a heavier weight. These cheating tactics will not make you grow more rapidly or become stronger, but they will place harmful stresses on your joint structures. Remember when we yanked on the Silly Putty? It got stiff and brittle. Your muscles, tendons, and ligaments will do the same with rapid force applications. Jerking the weight around will lead to muscle shortening, decreased range of motion, and loss of flexibility. More experienced weight lifters, especially athletes who rely on explosive strength, may use lighter weights and rapid power movements without detriment as long as they stick to the biomechanical guidelines detailed in this chapter. For instance: warm up before starting; stretch; use the full range of motion; and don't use momentum if your joint is in a mechanically compromised position.

Strains and Sprains

The injured tendon or ligament is analogous to an overstretched spring. When these tissues are stretched beyond a certain threshold, they become damaged and will not recoil fully. Ligaments are relatively avascular structures. Because their blood supply is poor, they heal badly and often don't return to their original length or strength following an injury. Individuals who have suffered a seriously sprained ankle will attest to the ease with which reinjury occurs. With the common "inversion sprain," where the outer part of the foot turns under, there may be a permanent ligamentous laxity on that side of the ankle. It becomes a vicious cycle: with each repeated sprain the ligaments become more stretched, the ankle becomes increasingly unstable, and the likelihood of reinjury escalates.

Initial care of a sprain should include nonsteroidal anti-inflammatory drugs (such as aspirin, ibuprofen, or naproxen), ice, and immobilization with either a cast or by taping or splinting. Aggressive physical therapy with muscle-strengthening exercises targeted at the affected joint can often prevent recurring injuries. If the joint remains unstable, many active individuals are able to return to their sport with the aid of a brace. If the condition is not amenable to bracing, there are often surgical alternatives. For example, lateral ankle reconstruction involves moving a tendon from the foot to the outside of the ankle, where the tendon is used to bolster the strength of the stretched ligaments. Long-term results of this procedure are generally very good.

Things to Keep in Mind When Starting a New Activity

If you are sedentary and wish to adopt a new workout regimen, be aware that the ligamentous laxity and muscle atrophy secondary to inactivity will render your joints vulnerable to injury. Even if you are currently active, taking up a new sport will probably involve using muscles and joints in untested and different ways. For example, if you are an avid swimmer and decide to take up running, consider that you are subjecting the structures that comprise your ankles to hundreds of pounds per square inch of pressure with each stride. Any instability will contribute to microtrauma, pain, and inflammation. Before undertaking a vigorous running program, first work to strengthen the muscles and ligaments that stabilize your ankles. You may want to start slowly by performing calf raises and walking (not running) stairs and hills. After two to three weeks of ankle conditioning, try running on a forgiving surface like wood, dirt, sand, or grass. You should never run on concrete or asphalt, as the inflexibility of these hard surfaces will produce unhealthy stresses on your knee and ankle joints, not to mention your lower back.

This material originally appeared in the April 1999 issue of Martial Arts Illustrated.

Cross-Training with Sport *Tae Kwon Do*

June Castro

Cross-training is an important element in any athlete's workout because it offers the muscle fibers in the body a chance to react to different stimuli. As a result, varying your workouts will effectively develop all facets of the body equally. Many professional athletes credit their high level of physical condition to a cross-training regimen. For the martial artist, it offers many benefits aside from improving the major components of fitness, which include cardiovascular endurance, muscle strength, and flexibility. Cross-training also develops and improves specific attributes such as stamina, agility, speed, explosiveness, timing, coordination, and relaxation.

Whether you are training for an athletic event or just trying to shed a few pounds, cross-training will prevent burnout and avoid overtaxing specific muscle groups. Repetition may be the mother of skill, but if your workouts are boring and monoto-nous, chances are your training sessions will become few and far between. Cross-training will keep your workouts fun, exciting, interesting, and more productive, thus enhancing your overall fitness and performance level.

Tae Kwon Do Goes to Camp

Actor Michael Guerin recently invited me to visit a sport *Tae Kwon Do* day camp in which his goal was to cross-train. Michael has had leading roles in five feature films and has been able to capitalize on his martial arts background with starring roles in *Kick of Death* and *Reflex Action*. He's also appeared in a number of commercials and print ads.

"Staying fit is an intrinsic part of being an actor, because at any given moment you can be called upon to use that part of your instrument which is your physicality. Whether it be a swimwear advertisement, a Levi's commercial, or an action movie, you must stay fit in this town to remain competitive," according to Michael.

Besides being a martial artist, Michael is an outstanding athlete. Throughout high school he was an all-star pitcher in baseball. In football he was a starter on both the offensive and defensive teams. Michael was also a recipient of a prestigious award presented for excellence in academics and athletics. He was a collegiate wrestler, and was the number-one golfer at the University of Rhode Island (a Division I school). Today, he still plays a decent game with a five handicap. Born and raised on the east coast, he is also an accomplished skater, hockey player, and triathlete.

As an athlete, Michael credits cross-training as a major factor in attaining his fitness goals. "Even with a background in the martial arts, I am continually searching for new and exciting ways to train. I love variety in my workouts and therefore look for opportunities to cross-train. When asked by a good friend to train with some Olympic hopefuls at a *Tae Kwon Do* day camp, I jumped at the chance."

The Ultimate Sport Tae Kwon Do Camp in Agoura Hills, California, offers a great cross-training opportunity for all skill levels. The training is conducted under the supervision of former United States national *Tae Kwon Do* team members Scott Fujii and Justin Poos. Although the main focus of the camp is high-level training for sport *Tae Kwon Do* competition, everyone is welcome. "If someone is not experienced in the art of *Tae Kwon Do*, they will still receive the necessary instruction and attention at their level to propel them further," says Scott.

With both outdoor and indoor training sessions scheduled, I was told, "rain, sleet, or snow," the camp would commence at 8:00 A.M. What followed was a comprehensive and intense seven-hour training program that included endurance and stamina conditioning; flexibility training; and footwork, distance, and coordination drills; fighting strategies; mental preparation; and, of course, various kicking combinations and training techniques.

A Typical Day at Camp

Shortly after arriving at the camp the participants venture out on a three-mile run, which includes intermittent sprints. After returning to the camp base, the participants are taken through an extensive stretching routine. Everyone is encouraged to work at his or her own level with an emphasis on breathing and proper alignment. To say the least, flexibility is definitely enhanced during this phase of the training.

The next session included practice of various kicking techniques. Each kick is thoroughly explained in theory and then well demonstrated to show practical application. Participants then practice the kicks in front of a mirror, with the primary emphasis on footwork and proper execution. The same kicking combinations are then applied on focus pads and kicking shields. In addition to training specific drills, common fight situations are isolated to work on counters and strategies. The training in this section enabled the participants to improve coordination, agility, accuracy, speed, and timing.

After a one-hour lunch break, the participants convened for sparring. Protective equipment is required to ensure safety. Although everyone is encouraged to partake in this section of the program, sparring is optional. "Since we have beginners as well as national champions in attendance, we try to provide a comprehensive, safe, and fun environment for all skill levels," explained Scott.

Participants spar for three-minute rounds with a one-minute rest in between. In this section, regardless of size, gender, or skill level, everyone gets a chance to spar with everyone else. Contact was light to medium with the emphasis on accuracy, timing, stamina, strategy, and control.

After fifteen rounds of sparring, which is an immense feat in itself, the participants are taken through circuit training. Using two-minute intervals with only thirty-second breaks, students rotate from station to station. The various stations include skipping rope, heavy bag work, shadowboxing, footwork drills, and plyometric exercises.

So after a morning run, two hours of footwork and kicking drills, an hour of sparring, and another hour of circuit training, how else can one be tortured . . . I mean, challenged? How about an hour of running hills! Not upgrades—*mountainous* hills. This is the "Rocky Balboa" part of the program. It was definitely a test of physical and mental strength, even if only revealed to oneself. One of the toughest fighters I know once told me, "To be a champion, you must train like one!" That was certainly apparent watching every runner make it up every hill.

The final section of the training involved upper-body conditioning and abdominal work. Variations of the familiar pushup were done to work different areas of the chest, shoulder, and triceps muscles. The abdominal phase included a progression for the various fitness levels in attendance.

What I found very impressive at this camp was not only the high caliber of instruction offered, but that both instructors drilled and trained right alongside the participants. It was also refreshing to see that egos were left at the door, and that there was mutual respect and camaraderie among everyone.

The Ultimate Sport Tae Kwon Do Camp offers quality instruction in a relaxed yet focused atmosphere. The workout is challenging, rigorous, and empowering. Is the camp for everyone? No. But if you're a champion in the making, a weekend warrior, or a martial artist seeking to expand your arsenal of training methods and fighting concepts, or if you're just looking for a new and challenging cross-training opportunity, this camp will certainly take your training to a higher level.

This material originally appeared in the June 1998 issue of Inside Karate.

16

101 Asian Secrets for Health and Beauty

Eric Lee

Maintaining a fresh, positive outlook on life is the best way to stay strong both inside and outside. If a person has a healthy body and a healthy mind, he will feel secure and happy about himself.

Good health and longevity have always been important topics. While there's no escaping the passage of time, we can prevent, delay, and even reverse the effects of biological age through the many options at our disposal, including cosmetic surgery and anti-aging techniques, theories, drugs, nutrients, and cosmetics.

When I was a youngster in Hong Kong, my father ran two herb shops. Our family lived in the back of one of them. A patient would come to the shop, where the doctor would examine him, make a diagnosis, then give a formula to the chef, who would prepare the mixture, which the patient would ingest on the spot. It was a good experience for me, and I learned a lot. Herbology is natural and good for cleansing, healing injuries, building strength, and detoxifying.

National Art of China

The art of healthy living in China has evolved over thousands of years. According to *The Yellow Emperor's Canon of Medicine*, people well acquainted with the way in remote times followed the principles of yin and yang, practiced bodybuilding exercises best suited to their own conditions, were temperate in food and drink, maintained a strict daily regimen in life, and did not overexert themselves. That is why they remained in good physical and mental condition, enjoyed naturally endowed life spans, and died only after the age of 100.

Life expectancy in the United States has been traced from an average of forty-seven years in 1900 to its current seventy-five years. Women can expect to live about eight years longer than men. I have many Chinese friends over seventy. One is a Daoist master who married a woman half his age and had a child at age seventy. Another is a pulmonary expert and herbal *chi kung* doctor, my adopted mother. I received straightforward and simple advice from another friend in his nineties for staying young: "Take it easy."

Youth is a feeling about yourself and your life that has nothing to do with age. It is a spiritual quality. To regain our youth we must change our thoughts, wake up our minds, and develop the consciousness of a child. If you worry about age and dwell on your birthdays, it makes you unhappy—and that is terribly aging.

And then there is beauty. The biggest changes in the perception of beauty today include courage, intelligence, and vitality. If a person has a healthy body and a healthy mind, she is going to feel secure and happy with herself.

What should a person do at the different stages of life to stay youthful? The answer is obvious. You must keep up healthy skin, hair, and body. Your mind and psyche must be healthy, too. When you feel better, you look better. Beauty is a natural by-product of radiant health. It vibrates from the inside. You can't

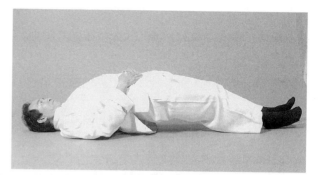

Special exercise for the back: keep elbows, shoulder, and upper back touching the floor. Elevate hip and lower back up and down.

be beautiful if you don't feel healthy and haven't worked at maintaining your optimism about life, your enthusiasm, and your intelligence.

What is fresh and new and youthful is how a person feels when his mind and body are in great shape. Think of it as adopting a holistic approach to beauty. You also want to make sure that the outside, which reflects the inner you, is as attractive as possible.

The three most important things for life are *chi* (energy), *jing* (essence), and *shin* (spirit). The basic elements of youth and beauty are diet, exercise, and rest and relaxation. We live in a fast-paced, MTV-inspired, computerized society. We are constantly exposed to toxins in our food and in our air. We must relax or the body will run down, especially if one is a workaholic. When we die it is because we have exhausted our essence.

Nutrition and exercise are the two most important physical factors influencing longevity. The two

Stretching

work together, with exercise helping bring nutritional components to all the body's tissues, enabling the tissues to use them fully.

Temperance is another secret for ancient centenarians. Nothing is overdone. This includes eating little, following a mainly vegetarian diet and eating only a limited amount of meat, drinking tea, and taking herbal and animal-based tonic medicines.

Food Therapy

Many people eat food according to taste and miss out on many nutrients the body needs to function properly. The Chinese see food as a form of therapy. It can maintain health, prevent diseases, slow aging, and strengthen the physique.

I drink juices from fresh vegetables for life energy and vitamins. Leafy green vegetables are high in chlorophyll. Fruit is good for detoxifying the blood. Noni, a Polynesian fruit, is good for promoting health. For hundreds of years it has been used as a preventative and a cure for a variety of ailments.

Another important aspect of nutrition and longevity is the role of antioxidants like beta-carotene, vitamins E and C, sulfur, amino acids, and selenium (found in brewer's yeast). They retard the aging process by inhibiting harmful environmental

influences and by preventing the degenerative process. They also slow down hardening of the arteries and loss of suppleness in body tissues.

Avoid salty foods. Food that is too salty shortens the life span as indicated in *Maxims for Preserving Life* by Bao Sheng Ming.

Smoking

Smoking burns the yin of the lungs, causing people to suffer from sore throat. It consumes the blood and shortens the life span. To banish the smoking urge, a book titled *Give Up Smoking* (published in the Qing dynasty) recommends steaming four ounces of perforated raw bean curd and topping it with two ounces of brown sugar until the sugar melts, then drinking the sweetened bean curd for three days.

The Functions of Tea

Some claim that tea makes you beautiful, and others say that it makes you smart. Tea's greatest benefit is digestive. When the body labors to digest a rich, fatty meal, less *chi* is available for breathing, thinking, and maintaining a steady heartbeat. Poor digestion increases stress.

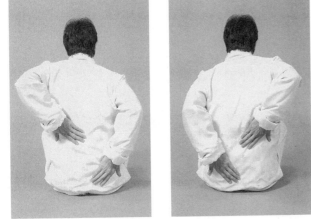

Massage for the kidney area: rub with palm of hand up and down thirty-six times.

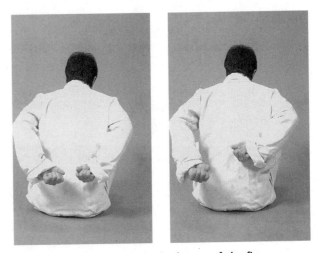

Tapping the kidney with the back part of the fist

I have been drinking green tea all my life. Tea promotes saliva secretion, quenches thirst, makes one strong and exhilarated, helps digestion, and dissolves greasy foods. It helps cure common colds, reduces weight, prolongs life, invigorates thinking, and strengthens memory. Finally, it is a source of vitamins C and E, especially wulong tea. Chrysanthemum tea is very good for brightening and strengthening eyes.

Physical Activity

The ancient Chinese realized that life lies in motion. "Running water is never stale and a door hinge never gets worm-eaten," as stated in *Lu's Almanac* by Lu Shi Chun Qiu. Physical activity improves the function of various organ systems, including the heart, allowing it to get more blood to the brain more efficiently and improving circulation. Exercise reduces the heart-beat and blood pressure, helps remove toxic substances from the body, burns off fat, reduces the body's susceptibility to many diseases, and is good for mental health. Physical activity has also cured insomnia.

Muscles are fibrous. Stretching prevents muscles from shrinking and keeps them warm, supple, and elongated. And, along with cardio-based exercises, stretching helps maintain strength and endurance. I enjoy exercise and have been doing *chi kung* since my youth. *Chi kung* cultivates essence, produces energy, and keeps the spirit in motion. Massage is natural and reduces energy blockage. I also recommend isometrics.

Breathing is of primary importance. When most people breathe it is very shallow. Singers know to breathe from the diaphragm. Breathing helps release toxins, promoting better health. Sleep and relaxation are crucial for helping boost the immune system. When you are relaxed, your *chi* will flow.

Standing meditation pose: keep palms up, tongue touching the roof of the mouth. Inhale and exhale slowly with the lower diaphragm.

Holding up the bucket pose: keep eyes closed, tongue at the roof of mouth, lips closed. Spread your legs and breathe from the diaphragm. Hold hands six inches apart.

Meditation pose: keep knees slightly bent, feet shoulder-width apart, tongue at the roof of the mouth. Imagine holding a small ball in the area of the diaphragm, one and a half inches below the belly button. Breathe slowly through the nose.

Warm palm: rubbing palms together brings *chi* to the area.

After palms have warmed, rub your palm sideways across your forehead. This improves facial circulation.

Facial massage: after palms have warmed . . .

. . . use hands to massage face in an upward, circular motion thirty-six times.

Rub the side of the ear gently to prevent wrinkles.

The Face

Your face is a reflection of who you are and what you eat, what you think, and what you feel. A shallow, dry, pale complexion is often caused by improper breathing and a lack of both fresh air and physical activity. Tension and dissatisfaction with life will also age the face. A smile is by far the best facelift. If you want your face to exude a healthy color and youthful appearance, you must supply nourishment to the tissues of your face. You can do this by stimulating circulation with a vigorous face massage. Also, proper breathing is mandatory as oxygen is the life link not only to a healthy face but a healthy outlook.

The skull massage will improve circulation.

Chin massage: upward motion with palms

Sitting meditation pose: with your hands six inches apart, imagine holding a ball.

Eye exercise: arm extended, focus your eye on your index finger as you bring your hand closer to your face.

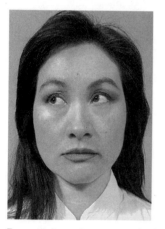 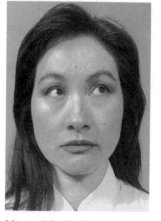 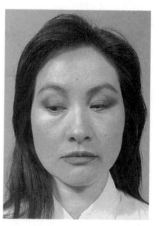

Eye training: close, open, look from side to side, look up and down.

The Mind

The single most overlooked factor of longevity is the psychological dimension. This includes prolonged and productive involvement in family and community affairs, and an acquired status of dignity and wisdom with a sense of the meaning and purpose of life itself. The harmony of the body and mind depends upon one's external life, the food one eats, the way one lives, the people one meets, the work one does, and the climate in which one lives. Attitude is a key to longevity.

The Canon of Medicine by Net Jing indicates that excessive emotion impairs the internal organs of the human body. "Anger hurts the liver, joy hurts the heart, brooding hurts the spleen, and melancholy hurts the lungs."

One must stay optimistic. All things negative will show one way or another. Release all stress. Always be peaceful in mind without vain hopes. Do not worry about personal gains and losses. Be kindhearted and patient. Distinguish between evil and virtue and between right and wrong. If you maintain this awareness, uphold integrity, and remain clearheaded, you will naturally be free from worries and troubles. A folk saying goes, "A good laugh makes one ten years younger; worry turns the hair gray."

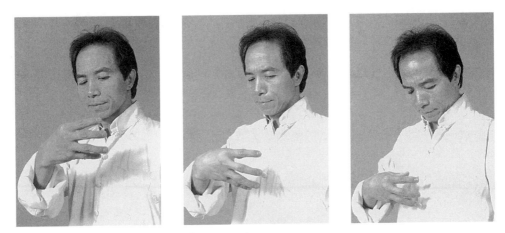

Upper body massage: lightly tap the upper chest area.

Hold the palms together with arms extended. Keep your eyes on your hands as you twist and wave your body like a willow.

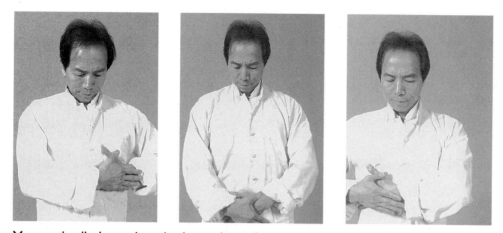

Massage the diaphragm in a circular motion, palms on top of one another.

Tap the pressure point at the lower extremities to improve circulation.

Massage for the bottom of the feet, palms facing feet

Massaging the knee area

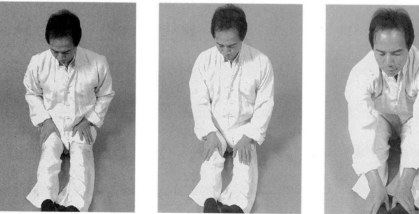

Massaging the length of the legs to improve circulation

It is our responsibility to take care of ourselves. We can be encouraged to take steps, but we cannot just *think* about it. Take the time to plan physically, psychologically, socially, and financially for a long, healthy life. It will enormously increase the odds that this will happen. Remember, a turtle goes nowhere unless he sticks his neck out. No one can live forever, but the life span of 100 years is within the reach of almost anyone who practices the traditional Chinese art of healthy living. Action produces results.

This material originally appeared in the October 1998 issue of Inside Kung-Fu.

The Secret Order of *Jing* (Monk Power)

Shi Yan-Ming and Allan David Ondash

Stance training uses natural movements in the most powerful way from the bottom up. Here, Shi Yan-Ming shows the proper position of the feet and knees in one of *kung fu*'s major power stances: the horse stance.

First, the good news: *jing*, or power, can be found in virtually every Chinese martial arts system. Now, the bad news: most practitioners don't know what to do with it. Want more bad news? Even those who know about *jing* and try to harness it don't know how to use it. And even those who know how to use it often use it for the wrong reasons or in ways that reduce its effectiveness.

The reason for this confusion of such a basic Chinese power supply is simple. We do not often see things as they are, we see things as *we* are. Many attempts have been made at the construction and reconstruction of true martial arts power, all without proper knowledge as a tool. Whatever one may find or think she has found in a fighting art cannot surpass the transcendental thought and physical studies attributed to a form of power so perfect that it has repeatedly and consistently proven itself for nearly

Bow and arrow stance

Tiger crouching

five thousand years. In fact, those who know the proper methods realize the only way they can be taken any further is through a study of internal practice.

It can be said that any practitioner who believes he may have taken on a new technique that is larger than *kung fu* will be surprised to learn he has simply borrowed a tiny piece. An alarming percentage of practitioners have not yet ventured beyond the first physical stage, proper turning of the feet. That is where we will begin.

Powering the Stance

Stance training utilizes the body's most natural movements in the most powerful way from the bottom up. The turning of the feet will always determine the direction of the body. It is important to verify that it is impossible to move the foot by itself. The foot always takes orders from the ankle, no matter what. Therefore, even though one's feet should be married wholeheartedly to the ground, emphasis on rotating the ankle, rather than (for example) pushing the heel outward, will immediately increase the initial power necessary to start a thunderous spiraling procession to the hands.

The perfect order of this bottom-to-top procession may be summed up as such: If one is walking

down a street and decides to turn at the corner, his head and shoulders do not move first in determining his new direction. He instead (naturally) turns his feet first, and the rest of his body obeys accordingly. Additionally, the lead foot points out the new direction before the second foot moves.

This brings us to a modern discrepancy worthy of clarification—*shaolin* versus *wushu*. In the movement art of *wushu*, both feet move lightly and almost always simultaneously so the practitioner can gather speed to block, strike, or kick. In the true fighting arts of northern and southern *shaolin*, the feet are more grounded to harness "shock power" in the waist for blocking, striking, or kicking, and so that the lead foot of every stance may be used to undermine an opponent's attack.

For example: Two opponents square off in horse stance postures. As the offender strikes, the defender simultaneously blocks and opens up the lead foot to a 45-degree angle. This invites the offender to step slightly beyond the defender's lead foot but unknowingly trap his own foot inside the defender's ankle. Then, and only then, does the defender spiral the rear foot into an explosive action that meets violently with the now-solid lead foot, causing shock power in the waist. The waist power is then linked to the striking hand, which hits the opponent like an iron whip and makes him simultaneously trip over the ankle lock.

Uprooting techniques such as ankle locks and leg throws are common to form application and self-defense. They work well against unseasoned fighters. However, when applying *san shou* in the ring against a fighter of equal caliber, uprooting would become a useless game of cat and mouse. Fighters use faster methods such as front-hand and front-leg maneuvers rather than the traditional reverse-hand, rear-leg applications. Some may misinterpret this as freeing oneself from the boundaries of traditional *kung fu* to demonstrate fighting just as *wushu* frees itself from tradition to demonstrate movement. This is simply untrue. The finest *san shou* masters always rely on the twisting shock power learned from traditional grounding of the feet. Without it, their techniques would suffer tremendously.

In light of this misconception, the Westerner may hypothetically compare *kung fu* to *wushu* by considering the difference between hockey and figure skating. In hockey, the players use hard, fast, and deceptive maneuvers with one goal in mind. Alternatively, figure skaters use soft, graceful, and telegraphed maneuvers with several specific goals in mind. Though both activities are practiced on ice, one is clearly more brutal than the other. Such is the case with *Shaolin* and *wushu*. Both have their rightful place in *kung fu*, but only one is deadly and the other is vaguely reminiscent of that deadliness.

Turning the Knee

Turning the knee is the second step in the procession of *jing*. As the ankle summons the foot into action, the knee should catch it and immediately help it on its way. Many injuries have occurred when practitioners either ignore the need for the knee to help or hyperextend it so far it blocks the *jing*. As a rule, the knee should never extend to a fully locked position. Additionally, when helping the *jing* upward, the knee should turn no farther than the angle of the issuing foot. In other words, it should always be placed in the middle between the rotating foot and the side of the waist that will be delivering the technique.

Separating the Waist

Next in this great procession comes the middle ground—the waist. According to *kung-fu* logic we are (externally speaking) halfway there. The presence of waist power is like the conceptual line that separates yin and yang. Without it, both would become one. Moving the waist before, or too long after, the foot is detrimental to *jing* and should be corrected. True waist power, like yin and yang, must unite with the rest of the body to become part of the whole, yet be separate enough to make a distinct difference. Many practitioners have trouble with, or simply do not train in, the separation of the waist. This often results in lazy or misleading forms of power. However, these issues can be corrected and advanced through the practice of simple waist-power exercises.

Begin separating the waist by starting from a straddle position with the feet held straight and arms relaxed. Next, lift the arms to shoulder level, bend them inward, and begin turning back and forth without moving the feet and using only the waist to keep the arms churning in a side-to-side motion.

Separating the waist: begin at a straddle position, arms relaxed (left). Lift the arms to shoulder level while bending them inward and begin turning back and forth without moving the feet (below left and right). Repeat in sets of twenty.

A second exercise uses stretching and isometrics as a means of freeing and strengthening the waist area. Starting from a relaxed forward stance against a wall (left foot leading), stretch the right arm out behind you at an upward 45-degree angle and place it flat against the wall. Next, grab the top of your right shoulder with the left hand and turn the waist and head as far as possible in the opposite direction. Hold for ten seconds and alternate.

Freeing and strengthening the waist: with your back in front of a wall, stretch the right arm behind you at an upward 45-degree angle, then grasp the top of your right shoulder with the left hand (above) and turn your waist and head as far as possible in the opposite direction. Hold for ten seconds and alternate (right).

The third exercise gives more attention to tilting the waist sideways. This is especially useful for side kicking. With the feet together and legs straight, interlock your fingers and stretch your arms straight above your head. Next, let the body slowly drop to one side while maintaining the straightest line possible from your hips to your hands. Hold for ten seconds and alternate.

The fourth exercise helps advance power in the waist. It is recommended that this exercise be practiced from a straddle position before attempting it from a power stance, or not until any proper positioning requirements have been thoroughly secured. Begin by mounting two five-pound sandbags to the sides of a firm weight-lifting belt. Then, from a straddle position with the hands held behind the

Tilting the waist: feet together and legs straight, interlock your fingers and stretch the arms high above your head. Next, let the body slowly drop to one side while maintaining the straightest possible line from the hips to the hands. Hold for ten seconds and alternate sides.

head and the feet straight forward, begin moving the sandbags from side to side using only the waist for power.

Pushing and Pulling the Shoulders

Next in line are the all-important shoulders. To effectively bring power to the hands, the shoulders must act exactly like a teeter-totter; you cannot push down on one side without causing the other to go up. For example, if the initial power from the foot is ultimately traveling to the right hand, you must not allow the right shoulder to pull the left. Instead, the left shoulder should pull backward at the same time and with the same amount of push from the right.

Advanced Method

Once a practitioner realizes how hard to push and pull on the shoulders without injuring himself, the advanced method can then be applied.

Just as we have noted that the foot cannot move by itself, we must realize the same holds true for the shoulders. When moving back and forth, as in straight punching, they are moved by the spine. As

Pushing and pulling the shoulders: *Sifu* Shi Yan-Ming uses a staff to demonstrate the proper positions of the head and shoulders in three power stances: bow and arrow (left), horse stance (center), and tiger crouching (right).

the power moves through the waist, it is then concentrated on the rotation of the spine, which in turn moves both shoulders, along with a relaxed neck and head, in an even and direct manner. A small shaft can spin a big propeller. Learn to internalize and concentrate on the mechanism, not the muscle.

The Elbow, Wrist, and Hand

As the swirling power leaves the shoulders, it races down the home stretch to the elbow, which ultimately pushes it through the wrist and to the hand. As a rule, the elbow should lead the wrist and never swing out of line with the target. The wrist should remain straight and relaxed, with the fist firm upon impact but never tense. Remember: muscle and tendon control is used only to lift the limbs and carry them to their destination. If you can punch or kick without tension, you have learned a valuable *kung-fu* lesson.

Putting Together the Puzzle

After properly identifying each piece of the *jing* puzzle, you will find it much easier to put together. You must follow the principle of yin and yang to obtain the correct result—though each movement is sepa-

rate, it must become part of the whole and all must end together. The foot must halt its rotation at the same exact time the hand strikes. You can think of this as a row of pearls lined tightly together, each marked the *foot, knee, waist, shoulders and head, elbow, wrist,* and *hand.*

If you tap the foot pearl first, the hand pearl will seem to move at the same time. That, however, is theoretically impossible. It is because of the procession of power from first to last that the hand pearl moves at all. Also, the harder the first pearl is hit, the faster and farther the last pearl will travel. This is the definition of true waist power. When executed properly, its effect almost seems unfair to an unsuspecting opponent—but in a life-threatening situation, the unfair goes home.

Shi Yan-Ming is a thirty-fourth-generation Shaolin Temple monk who owns and operates the U.S.A. Shaolin Temple in New York City and teaches kung fu, tai chi, chi kung, *meditation, and Chan Buddhism. Allan David Ondash is a twenty-year veteran of the* sil lum hung gar *system who teaches in Kingston, Pennsylvania. This material originally appeared in the August 1999 issue of* Inside Kung-Fu.

Healing the Body with the Mind

Daniel O'Hara

The founder of *pranic* healing, Grandmaster Choa Kok Sui.

The most beautiful experience we can have is the mysterious. It is the fundamental emotion which stands at the cradle of true art and science. Whoever does not know it and can no longer marvel, is as good as dead, and his eyes are dimmed.

—Albert Einstein

Wouldn't it be great to know how much internal power a *chi kung* teacher has before training with him? How about how balanced he is physically, emotionally, mentally, or even spiritually? What about having a way of measuring how much energy you have, or how your training is benefiting you? Not only does *pranic healing* teach you how to heal without touching, it answers these and many other questions that martial artists have.

When I was young, TV shows such as "Kung Fu," videos of Morihei Ueshiba, and stories of martial arts masters stopping bulls with a punch fascinated me. I wanted to explore and develop these mystical skills that were latent within me and waiting to explode like a Bruce Lee three-inch punch.

Like most youngsters starting in the arts, I began at the age of twelve, knowing that in under a month I would be able to walk on rice paper without a trace and make myself invisible, just as in the TV shows and stories. As I started my training in traditional arts, I learned *kata* after *kata*, got caught up in belt promotion, and put aside my dreams of being one with the universe and all the skills that went along with it.

Ultimate Stress Test

Thirteen years of training later, I found my dream. I had been a commodity trader for seven years and the stress tore me apart. All my years of studying numerous external training styles left me powerless against the stress I was under. I again searched out instructors to teach me about this mystical energy called *chi*. I tried a few big names, special programs, meditations, and even thought I knew something about Taoism. And still I hadn't felt *chi*, health, or the mystical experiences for which I had hoped.

Then it happened! My wife and I went to the Whole Life Expo, a place where hundreds of people were demonstrating everything imaginable. A sign at a booth proclaiming "Free Chakra Balancing" caught my eye. I didn't even know what a *chakra* was, but it was free. After I laid down on the floor, one of the students started moving his hands over me (about a foot away). I could feel waves of energy pulsing through me and I knew that everything I had dreamed about when I was a kid was possible.

For him to impart these ancient secrets to me, I thought I would have to sweep his floors for years. Much to my surprise, he said I could read a book called *Pranic Healing* and take a two-day class with a certified *pranic* healing instructor. Then I, too, could do this! I was so excited I almost didn't believe him. However, nothing could deny the experience so I gave it a try.

At the class, I met a remarkable certified *pranic* healing instructor named Master Steven Co, who could do things with his mind, like change the temperature of the room and heal others, with or without moving his hands in the air. Incredibly, in two hours I was feeling energy, projecting energy, and occasionally even moving people. I learned about *prana* (energy), how it affects the body, and the body's energy centers called *chakras*.

The Power of Energy

"The Meditation on Twin Hearts," the first meditation he taught us, felt incredible and sent energy running through me like I never thought was possible. In fact, it was too powerful for me, because I had high blood pressure. My previous training, unbeknownst to me, made my blood pressure worse and left me with my head racing with thoughts and unable to sleep at night. With *pranic* healing a relief was now in sight.

Within two weeks my blood pressure had normalized so I was able to do the meditation. My allergies and headaches disappeared and were replaced with a sense of peace that was unbelievable. My martial arts training rose to an even greater level. What a feeling to have finally found all that I was looking for—better yet, to know that I had two teachers who could and would show me everything I needed.

The founder of *pranic* healing, Grandmaster Choa Kok Sui, is the most amazing man I have ever met. He truly lives up to his title. His ability to move unfathomable amounts of energy and to easily explain the most difficult concepts is awesome. The first time I met him was in a class called "*Pranic* Psychic Self-Defense." We learned to make shields of energy that could protect someone from physical, emotional, and mental attack. Being a martial artist, I had heard about techniques such as iron shirt and others that would take years of meditation to develop. Within an hour we were hitting each other with objects.

Most people not familiar with energy would be astounded at how detrimental it actually is when someone is thinking negative thoughts toward them. For example, the expression "My ears are burning, someone must be talking bad about me" is based on the negative interaction of this energy. Through the eyes of people who see energy, it looks like red daggers hurled in the air toward the person, making his energy field hot and compact. Over time this could cause physical problems like shoulder pain or back pain, as in the expression, "Someone is stabbing me in my back."

Positive from Negative

Most people have probably experienced a negative energetic exchange, such as being in a hospital and then leaving feeling tired and depleted. *Pranic* healing can help martial artists protect themselves in all areas of life. One of the many things I love about Grandmaster Choa is that he frequently leads us in fun experiments. One night after class we were experimenting until the late hours of the night. I was ten feet away from Grandmaster Choa and trying to move him energetically. The mere thought of doing so resulted in a breeze across my face. As I put more energy into it, my feet started slipping backward, as if I were standing on ice and trying to push the Empire State Building. For my betterment, he had me continue trying to push him for another ten minutes. I was exhausted, but grateful for knowing that he allowed me a priceless opportunity to experience his energy and for me to develop my own.

That same evening I learned what was involved when "Grasshopper" (David Carradine in "Kung Fu") had to snatch the pebble from his master's hand. We had just completed learning a higher level of arhatic yoga, which is unwritten, internal Tibetan meditation.

A couple of us were snagging quarters out of each other's hands. Grandmaster Choa walked up with a man in his seventies named Pepe, who didn't know what we were doing, for he had never seen the game before. Grandmaster Choa explained the rules to Pepe and told him to take the coin out of my hand. I put my hand out, expecting to humor the man. He effortlessly stole the quarter out of my hand. In my mind, since I was forty-plus years his junior and had very fast hands, this must have been beginner's luck or I wasn't ready for him. Much to my surprise, he took it from me again and again.

Shocked and a little frustrated, I tried to take it away from him and got air every time. All of us were awestruck at how this could have happened. Grandmaster Choa then explained that since Pepe had been practicing a higher level of meditation than I, and since we had just finished meditating, his body had more *chi* and could move much faster.

This demonstration explains how someone older and trained in the internal arts can easily overcome the size, speed, and strength of youth.

Another night, we were having dinner after class when Grandmaster Choa picked up a lemon and asked me to suggest a different flavor for it. Like other advanced yogis of India, he transformed the bitter lemon into divine-tasting chocolate. He then energized my right index finger. The energy from the finger expanded from about six inches to at least six feet and continued to grow. With his energy in my finger, I touched several people from a distance and they felt the touch. To complete the evening, he made the room smell like roses and everybody felt better. If I hadn't experienced this with my own eyes and nose, it would have been hard to believe.

Healing for Martial Arts

Pranic healing is helping martial artists to become more complete (that is, to cultivate more energy and

Demonstrating sensitivity on the arms—sticky hands while touching.

to balance one's energy centers). For example, a *wing chun* practitioner's sensitivity, whether or not she knows about energy, is due to her inner aura becoming sensitive to energy. The level-five black belt test in *tai-jutsu* (*nin-jutsu*) training is the famous sword test given from behind. Here again, it is the sensitivity of the aura to oncoming energy that allows one to move out of the way before the attack. Grandmaster Choa has demonstrated movements in the martial arts that, when combined with energy, are devastating.

In the 1980s, Stephen Hayes's *nin-jutsu* was the rage, and rightfully so—it is a great art. In the 1990s, the Ultimate Fighting Championship brought grappling into the martial artists' repertoire, again making us all well-rounded practitioners. However, as much fun as kicking, punching, grappling, and getting faster can be, it is minute in comparison to healing someone's sprained ankle and helping him walk. The next level of training is mastering internal energy, which is *pranic* healing.

We have a saying: "Everything is energy," so the more you have, the faster you can be and the more rapidly you can heal yourself and others. I foresee a future of pro athletes and pro fighters having a *pranic* healer ringside, pumping them full of energy and eliminating and reducing injuries and recovery times. Martial artists will realize their dreams of training like the ancient masters.

When you look into the power of *pranic* healing, you can start at the top with Grandmaster Choa Kok Sui. With Grandmaster Choa's schooling as a chemical engineer, his success in business, and his humanitarian values, it is no wonder *pranic* healing is having such a profound impact on so many people. He has spent over twenty years studying Eastern and Western principles of meditation, martial arts, and other esoteric subjects, while continuously experimenting and validating their efficacy.

Grandmaster Choa has proven in his international lectures that people are ready to receive these ancient secrets to uplift humanity. He has earned a reputation for demystifying arcane principles and rituals into a pragmatic application relevant to this day and age. Seminars, healing centers, and foundations have been established in over forty-five countries to share these priceless teachings with humanity.

I have spent the past eighteen years studying many forms of external and internal martial arts. *Pranic* healing, while primarily a healing art, has improved every area of my life, especially my martial arts training. It is said that we use only 10 percent of our brain capacity. One of the reasons I took up martial arts was to develop greater powers of concentration and to stimulate other parts of my brain.

In the East they have a saying: "The mind is like a drunken monkey," meaning it is hard to control. Most people attempt a *tai chi* set to relax, but they can't. Their brains are racing. *Pranic* healing will teach students how to relax in minutes. The ability to focus the mind on one thing is also a valuable tool I have gained in my *pranic* healing training.

The professional fighter's ability to make a living will be greatly improved through *pranic* healing. Fighters lose money if they can't fight because of a training injury. Wouldn't it be great to speed up or altogether eliminate healing times?

When I met Joe Moreira for the first time, his knee was injured so badly he couldn't walk. Had I not intervened, he wouldn't have been able to teach a two-day seminar one day later. To further demonstrate how *pranic* healing speeds up healing times, in the advanced *pranic* healing class one of the students volunteers to cut himself. In most cases the healing time is reduced from one week to about ten minutes. A martial artist I know had a broken finger. A day earlier an X-ray clearly showed the finger to be fractured. I applied *pranic* healing on him. In ten minutes he was pain free and took off his splint. This rapid healing process is invaluable for today's warriors looking for an edge.

Many fighters look to supplements to increase their strength, speed, and power. Again, *pranic* healing will help in these areas. For strength, athletes take steroids. We have a natural solution to this harmful chemical process. It is called the master healing technique, and it floods the body with power. I have seen firsthand a bodybuilder who had maxed out on a bench press add another thirty pounds after I applied the master healing technique to him!

In the speed department, energy is again the key. I have seen Grandmaster Choa, who doesn't even work out, throw a punch so fast I could barely see only the recoil. *Pranic* healing will help fighters be stronger, move faster, and become more powerful.

The modern fighter will become more balanced externally as well as internally. The Taoists have a saying that if you are breathing heavily through the mouth, you should stop exercising. This belief was practiced since heavy exercise depleted the energy reserves stored in the *dan tian*. *Pranic* healing will teach fighters to replenish this internal gas tank or, better yet, have someone "in their corner" refresh them between rounds and during the fight. When fighters get tired, the cells in the body stop exchanging vital nutrients such as oxygen. Fighters train in high altitudes so their lungs will absorb more oxygen at normal altitudes. In *pranic* healing we use certain energies to dilate the lungs and air tubes to help people with asthma as well as fighters.

One attribute of a successful fighter is the ability to overcome pain. In hospitals doctors and nurses are using a no-touch healing method called *pranic anesthesia*. They are reporting results of almost no pain when inserting catheters and spinal taps. This same technique should be applied to reduce pain suffered in the ring.

The thoughts and emotions of a fighter can be a greater nemesis than the physical opponent. How does a fighter overcome the fear of fighting an opponent? Or, worse yet, the mental anguish of getting back in the ring after a loss? Surrounding the physical body is the energy body, which controls the physical health. After the energy body are the emotional body and mental body, which govern our emotional and mental health.

Pranic psychotherapy can help fighters overcome their fears, addictions, and limited thinking. I have seen people teach a seminar after complaining the day before that they couldn't walk, as with Joe Moreira.

It was Musashi who said, "The greatest warriors are those who are the greatest healers." In much the same way that Bruce Lee developed *Jeet Kune Do*, Grandmaster Choa has combined the essence of many healing and meditational modalities such as *chi kung*, *reiki*, and "laying on hands" to optimize and refine *pranic* healing.

Pranic healing is helping martial artists in over thirty countries learn how to heal and to develop all sides of the warrior and monk within us. In a two-day seminar, you will learn how to heal without touching, and make training injuries a thing of the past. Later, students are able to study arhatic yoga, unwritten Tibetan meditation.

Today, there are hospitals abroad that are medicineless and use *pranic* healing to treat cancer and other conditions. In the United States, hospitals and medical schools are now starting to teach and embrace *pranic* healing.

How to Learn

The best way to learn how to feel energy centers is in a *pranic* healing class. *Pranic* healing students are taught to test everything. To be able to do this the certified instructor will activate your hands and several energy centers, making energy easy to feel and use. Until your hands are activated, try this simple experiment to feel energy centers.

Put your tongue on your palate and smile; do fifteen squats; hold your hands out facing each other about six inches apart (as if you were holding a grapefruit); concentrate on your fingers and palms; do slow, deep diaphragmatic breathing for thirty to forty-five seconds.

The palm *chakras* (energy centers) with use or after activation become very sensitive. To feel (scan) a *chakra*, face your partner and move your hands from about five feet inward. As you move in, stop at the point where you feel pressure (if not, do the sensitivity exercise again) and you will feel the size of the *chakra*. These energy centers feel like subtle pressure or a magnet.

With time you will feel the movement and various properties of the *chakra*. You can feel a potential instructor's energy body and energy centers and see just how much he really knows.

Since *pranic* healing is a healing-based system for developing oneself spiritually, it is a perfect complement to balance the energy of most martial artists. If you were to scan the lower energy centers of most *chi kung* practitioners and most external martial artists, you should see that their lower energy centers are overdeveloped and the upper centers are underdeveloped. This puts great tension on the body's energy system and on the underlying physical body.

Therefore, you should seek balance in your life, training, and energy systems. *Pranic* healing will give you the skills to achieve this.

This material originally appeared in the January 1999 issue of Inside Kung-Fu.

The *nin–jutsu* sword test. Daniel's inner aura feels the oncoming blow (left and right).

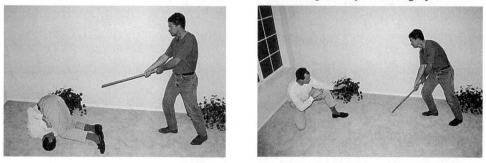

He rolls out of harm's way (left) and gets back into position (right).

19

Kam Yuen's
Secret to Eternal Health

Kam Yuen

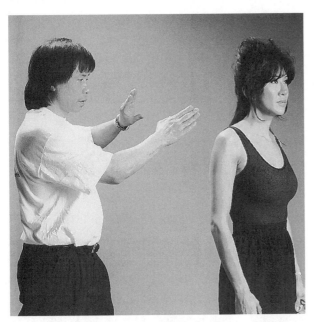

A big part of Kam Yuen's energetic healing method is learning to correct injury and illness yourself. Better yet, you can make disease and injuries a virtual impossibility with just a few minutes of practice a few days a week.

In all areas of human endeavor, phenomenal gains in knowledge are creating dramatic breakthroughs for all.

The breakthroughs benefit us every day and in almost every way. In this chapter, we will discuss how to use the most up-to-date knowledge of personal empowerment based on the wisdom and secrets of our ancient past. This new technology emerging from the distant past can instill new capabilities and talent in you by improving the way you use your mind and body to act, respond, and react.

In the middle of this technology is *martial arts energetics*, a spectacular breakthrough technique. Combining traditional *chi kung* techniques with the latest knowledge of physiology, biochemistry, quantum physics, and psychology can help you design a powerful self-changing methodology. This makes it surprisingly easy to achieve the changes and improvements needed for healing ailments.

In my thirty years of teaching martial arts, helping people realize their greater potential has always been my ultimate goal. Now I have a whole new set of powerful tools to help you and others. I want to share this with the martial arts community. It's time the general population recognized the martial arts for the benefits they can offer to humanity. It's time for the healing arts and the martial arts to once again become two sides of the same coin.

Miraculous Recovery

You will become increasingly impressed with the power of these new techniques, as I have been in using them with my patients and students. Usually a student or patient makes an astonishingly quick improvement, change, or recovery that had previously seemed impossible, or would have taken months of tedious therapeutic work or painstaking training using the latest state-of-the-art methods. Now I can help someone improve much more quickly and easily—most of the time, instantly.

For example, in a single session, a confused, lacking-in-confidence, depressed youngster gains all the confidence and action-packed motivation that's needed to have a career and purpose in life. Such improvement is common. This method is a revolutionary departure from the traditional ways of learning and bringing about change.

My desire is to make available the benefits of martial arts energetics to more people—not just to professionals, but to the general population, and especially to martial arts practitioners, to whom these benefits have always belonged.

These techniques will work for you if you choose to apply them to yourself and others. After learning them you can transfer their use to any life forms in need of healing. Once this technique is widely known, it will be commonly accepted and available at an affordable cost. You can gain skills and power over your life. It leads you to self-reliance and independence.

I want to inform and excite you regarding the enormous possibilities these techniques can have for you. Once you realize that you can apply these easy and powerful techniques yourself, you can improve any chosen areas of your life: physical, emotional, behavioral, intellectual, psychological, psychic, spiritual, and financial.

When I began to lecture on, demonstrate, and teach my audiences and students these techniques, I was frequently asked for written instructions or books on the subject. I could only refer them to traditional books and journals that were not of much help in the practical sense. They were mostly written with a lot of *chi kung* exercises and theories to develop and increase *chi*. Instead, we needed instructions written in a straightforward manner that could be followed by anyone.

My purpose is to reach a wide audience and let a great number of people benefit from these instant healing techniques. As a result, my articles are written to explain extremely useful methods from a self-help perspective. Martial arts energetics does not just give you intellectual understanding or mere "insight." Exact instructions are given for you to make the specific changes you want; scientific jargon is replaced with clear, everyday language. I will include easy-to-follow, step-by-step instructions and detailed examples of how others have used these techniques to enrich their lives. Here are a few of these techniques and explanations of what they can do for you.

Improving Goals

A few minutes is all it takes for you to make an energetic correction. The correction will activate your hidden powers and create an instant change. You can now easily fulfill your every goal and desire. Many people have used these techniques to finally achieve what they'd only dreamed of for years. Whether you want to market your creative talents, make a career change, or go on a diet, by using your *instant healing technique*, you'll never have to push yourself to do the job; instead, you'll have to remind yourself to stop using willpower! Use less willpower and more skill power to make corrections.

Improving Physical Skills

You can now master new skills and challenges. You can now use techniques better than those used by Olympic champions or martial arts masters. They have used similar techniques to achieve peak performance. You can actually correct, reprogram, and prime your mind to think more creatively, solve problems more effectively, and learn and apply new information quickly. Give yourself more confidence, raise your self-esteem, and increase your learning. You can use these techniques to become more dynamic and assertive and to master new skills quickly to achieve success more often.

Improving Health

You can now direct your own personal healing procedure to illness and injuries. Along with your doctor's supervision, you can help yourself get well—quickly. Based on recent scientific research on the power of positive thinking in healing disease—even cancer—this technique often works where conventional medicine fails. Better yet, you can prevent possible diseases and injuries, even making them an impossibility. A highly stressed businessman used it to ease the symptoms of his irritable colon. Just a few minutes of practice a day for a few days can actually help promote health and vitality and reverse illness and injury.

Change Yourself Overnight

You can activate your innate ability to change yourself. You can refine your own technique and be more effective by practice and application of energetic cor-

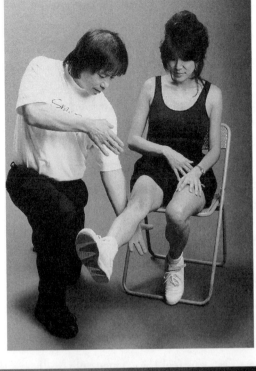

Many of Kam Yuen's treatments are performed without the aid of physical contact. It astonishes many, until they discover how well it works. This woman suffered from tendinitis of the elbow, knee, and ankle that created constant pain. After several sessions, she not only was pain free, she could resume her love of tennis.

rections to yourself. You can do it with ease and safety. You can erase pains and aches resulting from illness and injury. You can increase your powers of concentration and reinforce the new skills you've found. Remember, you can use this technique to improve any areas of your life, even to erase fears and phobias.

Learning to Make Energetic Corrections

To begin, you must learn to feel the change in energy. Learning to feel it can only be achieved by practicing how to feel it. Everyone basically knows how it feels to have "high" or "low" energy. To the Western mind, "energy" remains an abstract term to describe an invisible life force that cannot be measured by conventional technology. In ancient times, martial arts masters qualified and categorized the many levels of energy that enliven the human body. They accepted the invisible forces that animate and make us strong or weak. They learned by experience to distinguish between them, and finally to influence them with their own mental and energetic techniques. Today I rely upon those ancient discoveries to deal with the causes of modern illness and injury.

At first you feel the changes physically. As you practice how to distinguish this feeling, you will evolve into feeling the changes mentally. Remember that whatever you do and feel physically can also be accomplished mentally.

You need only to accept the existence of energy, be connected with it, and use it. The energy of change is available to anyone who is aware of that possibility. The results do not require an acceptance by your belief system or any act of faith. As mentioned, it is something we all have; all it takes is a desire and the process of learning how. There is nothing esoteric about it; there is nothing to fear. This method is practical, down-to-earth, and humanistic. It's like learning how to use a computer; anyone can eventually learn if shown how.

As previously mentioned, the disconnection of energy causes disruption and disturbances that can affect any level of your being. It makes you weak and lowers your resistance and protection, which leads to ailment, disease, and injury. Distress or injury experienced in one part of your body can create disturbances or weakness in other parts of your body. The exact causes of the disconnection need to be identified.

A practitioner of this energetic methodology can pinpoint exactly when and where the disconnection occurred. A precise correction can then be made so your energy vibration is less affected by negative influences. Your health and the way you think and respond to the circumstances of your life can be positively changed by knowing how and where to direct the energy.

The practitioner, as you might expect, has a unique view of health and disease. Disease is never considered to be simply caused by microbes and germs. Injury is not viewed as being caused by incorrect physical actions or unexpected impacts. Strength and weakness, disease and wellness, are seen as opposites of the same unifying conditions in life. They are not separable, but equal and opposite, making up the whole as symbolized in the figure of the yin and yang.

Many practitioners in the *chi kung* circles erroneously think that energy diminishes with age until it is used up and then we die. They also think a single energy source makes up a person's life force, and it's the blockage of the flow of energy that causes disease and distress. Years of countless *chi kung* exercises are frequently recommended. They practice just to feel their own *chi*. The healing energy for changes is expected to come mainly from the *chi kung* exercises. *Chi kung* exercises will help with the balancing and feeling of the *chi*, however, I do not feel that merely balancing and developing the general feeling of the *chi* will always give every person good health and instant recovery from injuries.

When you learn this technique, you are in charge, essentially, of your whole life. You gain insight and become your own expert. This will empower you as martial arts training does. No longer will you completely and blindly depend on others to be your experts. It is of paramount importance for your own survival. After you learn these techniques, you own the tools and the knowledge to take charge, and gain self-expertise and self-mastery.

Following are some strength and weakness drills you should practice. Practice until you know exactly how it feels to be strong and exactly how it feels to be weak, energetically speaking. Learn to distinguish the feeling when you strengthen or weaken another person just by changing the way he stands and moves as you muscle-test him. When he stands with his toes turned out, he will lose strength. Standing with his toes turned in, he instantly gains strength. When you see people walking with their toes or feet turned out, they unconsciously weaken themselves. Their internal energy constantly gets depleted. They may wonder why they feel weak and fatigued. Turning the toes in creates a stronger muscle response when a strength test is done, whereas turning the toes out weakens the response. In martial arts training there is a practice of standing in a pigeon-toed stance to develop overall strength.

In energetic testing we have the person make spherical or circular movements standing with her toes out. The spherical movements strengthen the weakness of the turned-out position, whereas without the movements, the person would respond weakly.

In the gym many of the movements that are commonly used weaken a person's energy field. For example, biceps curls and arm extensions actually weaken the person instantaneously. By performing spherical movements, you instantly become stronger without using any more effort to achieve strength. Becoming fatigued, often in a vain attempt to increase your capacity to do more physically, is not the best way to get stronger.

Most exercises done in the name of aerobic exercises are actually anaerobic exercises; they make a person more fatigued. You get out of breath doing those exercises; true aerobic exercises do not get you out of breath. Jerky and choppy movements are also anaerobic because they deplete your aerobic capacity.

Philosophy of Tension

Modern society insists that nothing worthwhile is obtained without grueling, extraordinary effort, day in and day out. Whether climbing the corporate ladder or losing weight, we are told that success only comes through massive amounts of time, blood, sweat, and tears. Thus, we have trained ourselves to be tense and aggressive. This makes it difficult to feel the change in energy, since ideally you should be in a relaxed state of mind trying to accomplish goals.

Less Effort Is More

In nature, water and air are carried along effortlessly to create the greatest strength. We can train our minds and our bodies to emulate the immense forces of nature. By practicing effortless movement in exercise and thought, you open your physical and creative energies to accomplish many times more than you ever thought possible through straining and tension.

Physical Strength Versus Energetic Strength

Bodybuilders are a classic example of physical strength. They have disciplined themselves to pump iron to build enormous muscle mass and impressive definition. It may be easily shown, however, that even a basic knowledge of energy channels and flow can expose glaring weakness in the most Herculean behemoths. Thus, learning the flow and use of energetic strength has clear advantages for health and recovery from injury.

Circular Motions Versus Linear or "Power" Motions

Raise one arm in front of you. Have a partner push down on that arm while you try to resist. The stronger person will overcome the other. Either your arm stays up or your partner will push it down. With your free arm, move your fingers and hands in small, circular movements. Imagine you are rolling golf balls in the palm and fingers of your free hand. Notice how the raised arm is much stronger the second time your partner pushes down on it. This illustrates how physical strength can be increased by using energy. Linear, back-and-forth movements decrease your strength while circular movements increase it.

The Strength of the Tongue

Have a person with his feet turned out place the tip of his tongue on the roof of his mouth. This will instantly increase his physical strength by enhancing the energy flow that physically connects the midbody meridians. Try the arm test again with the tip of the tongue lying normally in the mouth. The response will be weaker. Test again with the tongue raised to the roof of the mouth. Placing the tongue at the roof of the mouth instantly strengthens a person and eliminates weakness.

Standing with Toes in and Out

Standing with the toes pointed out, the person will respond weakly in a muscle test. Turning the toes in will instantly get a strong response. This is the beginning method for gaining the feeling of a high or strong energy response, and a corresponding low or weak energy response.

Centering

Placing a hand vertically along the midline of the body will increase strength. When the body and focus are centered, the body is stronger. Placing a hand anywhere else will weaken the body.

Balance and Stabilization

Standing erect is stronger than leaning too far back or too far forward. Standing up straight must be done effortlessly. The stability of your legs comes from looseness in your feet, ankles, knees, and hips. Strength of the upper body comes from the stability of your foundation, which is your feet and legs.

The practice drills mentioned in this article provide the basic steps that will lead to your mastering the greatest healing skills currently known to humanity.

Kam Yuen has been one of the world's most recognizable kung-fu *figures for more than twenty years. After gaining fame as the soul behind the original "Kung Fu" television series, Yuen went back to teaching traditional Chinese martial arts. Today, he runs Shaolin West International in Canoga Park, California, as well as traveling the globe as the chief proponent of martial arts energetic medicine. This material originally appeared in the January 1998 issue of* Inside Kung-Fu.

20

Should You Build—or Buy— a Wooden Dummy?

Sean C. Ledig

The *mook jong*

Buy or build? That seems to be the question for practitioners of *wing chun*, *Jun Fan Gung Fu*, or *Jeet Kune Do* when it comes time to get a *mook jong*.

Buying one would seem to be the simple solution. No fuss, just send a check or money order, or break out with the plastic and in a few weeks you'll have your own wooden dummy. But how many of us have the $300 to $1,000 or more to spend on a piece of training equipment, especially if you're struggling to raise a family and still have enough money left over to pay for the lessons to learn to use the dummy?

Building one would seem to be the simple answer to that problem, but where do you begin? Where do you find a decent set of construction plans? Where do you find the body? How do you make the arms and legs without buying a set of expensive tools to rival that of Norm Abrams? And where do you find the time to make the dummy without cutting into your job, your training schedule, or your family life?

Let me tell you how I did it.

Getting the Plans

My first problem was locating a set of plans for building a dummy. Unfortunately, while your local hardware store might have the entire Black & Decker library, you won't find the plans for a *mook* there. Whenever I mentioned to the sales clerk what I was trying to build, I usually got one of two replies:

- "Huh?"
- "Hey, you know kerotty? Cool! I was a yellow belt before I quit. Maybe we could get together and practice sometime."

After ditching that guy somewhere near the power tools, I drove to my friend Andy's house. Andy had a copy of Leung Ting's massive volume on *wing chun* that had diagrams for a "live" dummy, which is supported by wooden beams or springs, and a "dead" dummy, which goes straight into the ground like a telephone pole.

Overall, it is a good book about *wing chun* and a must for any practitioner's library, but it was missing the dimensions of the project. Failing that, I pored over my collection of books and magazines, but could not find the dimensions of the dummy. Instead, I studied the pictures as closely as I could, trying to find a point of reference so I could calculate my own measurements.

I found what I was looking for in James Lee's classic *Wing Chun Kung Fu*. On one of the last pages is a picture of either James or Bruce Lee, practicing an *osoto-gari* type of throw with the dummy. Knowing that both men were about five feet seven inches (my height), I was able to calculate approximate measurements for everything except the distance between the tips on the top two arms.

My friend Tony, *Jeet Kune Do sifu* and computer nerd extraordinaire, located an excellent set of construction plans, complete with measurements, on the Wing Chun World website at www.wingchun.org /pics.html. Since I do not like to take credit for another's work, I would strongly advise the reader to get on the Net and download a copy.

Procuring a Body

My first attempt to build a *mook* was about a couple of years before the one I have now. The body was a section of an damaged eight-inch-by-six-foot telephone pole I found in the waste pile at a nearby lumberyard.

That pole was one of two things I did right in that first attempt. I trimmed the rough edges, bringing it down to five feet in length. I used generous amounts of insecticide to kill the termites that were starting to make a home there. I put a sanding disc on my power drill, smoothed the body, filled in the cracks with wood putty, sanded it again, and added a clear finish.

Contrary to what some instructors might tell you, it is not necessary to build the body out of some expensive, endangered tropical hardwood. Sure, it looks nice, but a serious martial artist is more concerned about the usefulness of his *mook*, not how pretty it is.

For the backyard martial artist, a telephone pole would be all that is needed. If anyone out there can break a telephone pole body, call me—I want to study with you. But as I said before, the telephone pole body is the only thing I did right. I drilled round holes for the arms and the leg, allowing them to spin upon impact. Also, when I had a professional woodworker make the arms, I wasn't clear in my directions. As a result, he made arms that looked good, but broke after a few uses. In addition, the top arms were too far apart.

The following year, I scrapped the dummy, returned to the lumberyard, and purchased a pole rather than rooting through their trash pile and taking my chances.

Making the Arms and Leg

The leg was nothing more than a seven and an eleven-inch long one-inch pipe section, joined by a 135-degree double female joint. The eleven-inch section went through the hole to create the dummy's leg. Outside the back of the dummy, I screwed a wall mount onto the end of the pipe, and screwed that into the dummy body. Be sure to use a drill for the screws to avoid splitting the body.

With that done, I took some pipe insulation, wrapped it around the leg, and fastened it with duct tape. This step is optional, but highly recommended if you don't want to develop crippling arthritis in your feet and ankles.

The arms were another story, since I did not own a lathe or know anyone who did. All the other tools I needed were ones I owned or were readily available for the taking in my father-in-law's garage.

I hit every equipment rental store in Hillsborough County, Florida, but none had lathes. They were, however, willing to rent me any type of backhoe, dump truck, or other heavy machinery I wanted. Obviously, none of the shop owners knew any of my former bosses from the U.S. Forest Service or they would know I'm even harder on other people's expensive machinery than I am on my dummy.

My wife suggested I check out some of the local high schools to see if I could use any of their shop equipment. Her idea worked, as I found that several local high schools had adult education classes in woodworking and metalworking. In addition, one local middle school hosted a woodworker's club two nights a week. For a small annual fee, I would have access to the shop, advice on using the equipment, and even some pretty good scrap piles I could rummage for the wood for my arms.

Mounting the Dummy

Making the square holes was the most difficult part of the job. This is where you will most likely want to break out with the plastic and make a call to one of the many companies that sell *mooks*. The only way to do it was to drill holes, then spend many hours with a hammer and wood chisel to make them square.

The way I got through it was to consider the hammering and chiseling part of my workout. It is a great way to build your triceps, key muscles for the *chum choi* or straight punches for which *wing chun* is famous.

After drilling and chiseling out the arm holes, the dummy was ready to mount. Initially, I planned to make holes through the top and bottom of the dummy for a pair of one-by-four slats to go through.

But then it hit me. Why not suspend it from springs? I looked through my lengthy collection of *Inside Kung-Fu* magazines, trying to get ideas for a spring-mounted model. Fresh with some new ideas, I returned to the local hardware store and purchased some large carriage bolts, two six-foot four-by-sixes, twelve sturdy eye-hooks, and about eight six-inch long heavy-duty rocking horse springs.

When I got the stuff home, I drilled holes about every sixteen inches, from the ground, in two lines about two feet apart on the concrete storage shed in back of my house. After hammering the cement anchors into the holes, I drilled more holes every six inches on each of the four-by-sixes, and bolted them into the wall.

Next, I drilled holes for four eye-hooks, two near the top, two near the bottom. To give the dummy a little more room to spring backward, I drilled the holes a little rear of the halfway line between front and back.

Following that, I drilled holes for eight other eye-hooks on the four-by-sixes, with one hole slightly above, and one slightly below its corresponding eye-hook on the dummy. Taking the rocking horse springs, I put two each on each of the dummy's eye-hooks. Then, putting the dummy on a cinder block to hold it up, I fastened the springs to the four-by-sixes and, violà, the dummy was ready to use.

One final point if you decide to make the dummy spring-mounted instead of suspended by slats or fixed straight into the ground. The plans from Wing Chun World recommend that the arm and leg holes have one-quarter inch of space in all directions to let the dummy have some "give" when you hit it. This is not as necessary if your dummy is spring-mounted; my replacement arms will fit more snugly next time. But like everything else in *kung fu*, you learn from experience and carry on.

NOT JUST FOR *WING CHUN* ANYMORE

No matter what style you practice, you can find plenty of uses for the wooden dummy. A *mook jong* is more commonly known in the martial arts world as a *wing chun dummy*. But once you've gone through the trouble of building your *mook*, you can use a little imagination to find applications for whatever other arts you've studied.

For example, in the back of James Lee's book *Wing Chun Kung Fu*, you can see someone practicing a throw similar to an *osoto gari* in judo. While you can't throw the dummy as you would your *uke* (partner), you can still practice the entries to many throws found in *judo* or other grappling arts. That single leg on the front of the dummy is a great place to practice a lot of your leg-hooking moves while grabbing onto the arms.

After awhile, you'll notice that your entries are much faster, and in practice with a partner you'll move much more fluidly. And entering in on your opponent is half the battle for any *judoka* or grappler.

Another favorite technique I like to practice on the dummy is a *silat* sensitivity drill my *Jeet Kune Do* instructor, Tony Chan, taught me. In that drill, you begin with a *guong sau* (scooping elbow-up block) with your right arm on the left-side dummy arm, step left, and follow that with a left straight punch to the body. Then, do a left *guong sau* to left-side arm, step around and do right and left straight punches, followed by a left vertical elbow, all between the two top arms.

Do a left *guong sau* on the right-side arm, step around, and do a right straight punch. Now, do a left *guong sau* on the right dummy arm and do everything you did already in reverse. For students of Filipino martial arts, the dummy also makes a good partner for practicing *hu bud* drills.

And speaking of Filipino arts, weapons arts—particularly *kali*, *arnis*, or even any of the traditional Chinese or Japanese weapons—can be used against the dummy. I enjoy using the dummy for practicing my *espada y daga* or single stick and knife techniques. I also find that the dummy is useful for developing the sticking energy with my *tai chi* sword.

A word of caution: you won't want to strike the dummy full force with your practice weapons, particularly rattan poles or sticks. It could shorten the life of your weapons as well as possibly damage the arms and body of your *mook*.

On the other hand, you shouldn't be afraid to make some moderate contact. After all, how often do you get to cut loose on your partner? Also, weapons students need to learn how to actually make contact with some hard surface if they aspire to be something more than baton twirlers. If it wasn't so pathetic, it would be a riot the times I've invited some *nunchaku* twirler to hit a heavy bag or tire *makiwara* and watched the weapon fly out of his hand.

Perhaps the most obvious applications besides *wing chun* techniques are those in *Jun Fan* kickboxing and *Jeet Kune Do*. That single leg sticking out at you simply begs to be hit with the side stop kick or the stepover side kick. Once you get proficient at closing the gap with either kick, work on your entries.

Try following up that kick with a knife slash (using a wooden knife, of course) or work on some trapping techniques with the arms. From trapping, try moving into some grappling. That lead leg is still out there, just waiting to be hooked, or even grabbed.

Once you become proficient at entering, trapping, and grappling with the dummy, when you go back to practicing with a live partner, he won't know what hit him.

Was It Worth It?

Though at times I didn't think so, I have to say "yes." I spent nearly five months of my free time, often taking me away from training. However, I would like to point out that when I started building the dummy, I was paying $100 a month to my *sifu*. While he was a good teacher, one I would highly recommend, I felt I wasn't retaining much of what he taught me since I had no one to practice with on days I didn't train with him. Having my own dummy at least gave me a means to practice when I couldn't train with him.

A dummy can also be used to practice other arts, particularly the Filipino stick and knife arts, as well as *hu bud* drills, according to my *Jeet Kune Do* instructor, Tony Chan.

The decision to build a dummy, however, owed more to a story one of my college economics professors told me about two men marooned on a desert island. One immediately sharpened a stick on a rock and used it to spear a single fish every day for his food.

The other man, however, took vines from the trees to make a net. Though he went hungry for several days while making the net, once it was completed he could catch many fish in a short time, and used the free time left over to think of ways to get off the island.

In short, sometimes it is better to put off a short-term advantage for a long-term gain.

This material originally appeared in the September 1998 issue of Inside Kung-Fu.

PART 5

Nutrition

21

Getting Lean and Staying There

Pay Heed to What You Eat

Christine Lydon, M.D.

The most ambitious training regimen in the world will not yield the results you hope for without proper attention to good eating habits. After age twenty, our metabolic rate slows by approximately 10 percent per decade and the importance of diet becomes even more evident.

Unfortunately, almost everyone seems to think that "eating right" is synonymous with "deprivation and suffering." This is simply not the case, or I wouldn't be able to pull it off. Believe me, I have a voracious appetite and a bad sweet tooth. But between my medical background and my experience in sports nutrition, I've always managed to develop diet strategies that enabled me to eat a lot of good-tasting foods and still stay lean.

You don't need an advanced degree to develop an intelligent approach to eating. Even if you don't know the first thing about physiology or nutrition,

it is necessary to obtain a basic knowledge of diet management. This should also include a review of the basic nutrients. This knowledge will make it possible for you to shed unwanted pounds and keep them off. The best part is, you won't feel like a martyr doing it!

Water

About 70 percent of the human body is made up of water. Water aids the liver and kidneys in the detoxification of poisons and the elimination of wastes from the body. The delicate balance of the body's electrolytes occurs in the water contained within and around the cells that make up all living tissue.

The importance of adequate fluid intake cannot be overemphasized. Without sufficient water, we become dehydrated and our organs (including muscles, liver, and kidneys) do not function optimally. Optimal kidney function leaves the liver free to perform maximum lypolysis (fat burning). In addition, proper hydration leads to enhanced thermoregulation and increased oxygen exchange in the lungs.

Simply stated, the well-hydrated individual will have greater endurance and a more comfortable workout. Water is also an excellent diuretic. Not only will high fluid intake increase urination, it will also decrease overall water retention and bloat. Since we do not feel thirsty until we are already in a dehydrated state, it is best to drink water with sufficient frequency to prevent thirst.

Most sources recommend that the active individual consume a minimum of one gallon of water per day. Although you may have to work up to this volume gradually over a week or so while your bladder adjusts, you will reap the benefits of your efforts almost immediately. Not only does water act as a natural appetite suppressant, but drinking water below your body temperature can actually help you to lose weight. Did you know that consuming one gallon of icy cold water will cause your body to liberate over 150 calories of energy? What a great way to burn fat!

Carbohydrates, Fiber, and Sugar

Carbohydrates contain four calories per gram and are the main energy source for the body. When three or more six-carbon sugar molecules are joined, the resulting molecule is known as a *complex carbohydrate*. One or two six-carbon sugar molecules linked together comprise a simple sugar. Complex carbs are further classified into *fibrous* and *starchy carbohydrates*.

Because fiber cannot be digested by the human gastrointestinal (GI) tract, it does not contribute calories and is passed as waste. It is, nonetheless, vital to good health. Inadequate dietary fiber leads to a sluggish GI tract, water retention, bloating, constipation, and an increased risk of developing colon cancer. In addition to being rich in vitamins, miner-

als, and antioxidants, fruits and leafy vegetables are excellent fiber sources and most references advise consuming at least five servings per day.

Typically, complex starchy carbohydrates are assimilated by the system more slowly than simple sugars and will provide constant and sustained (though less intense) energy levels. The lower the glycemic index of a given carbohydrate, the more gradually it will be digested into its components and absorbed from the GI tract into the bloodstream.

Less insulin is released from the pancreas over a given time in response to foods with low glycemic indexes. Hence, the body has more time to utilize the molecules for fuel, rather than storing them as fat. Whole grains, legumes, pasta, and yams are among the best sources of complex carbohydrates. Processed foods such as white rice and bread, and even nonprocessed foods like potatoes have higher glycemic indexes and are assimilated at rates similar to simple sugars. For this reason, they are more readily stored as fat.

When consumed, simple sugars like sucrose and dextrose provide a burst of energy that often gives way to lethargy. However, not all simple sugars are created equal. Fructose, the sugar found in fruit, is processed by the body in a manner similar to unprocessed complex carbohydrates. Due to the rate at which fructose enters the bloodstream to influence insulin levels, it is less easily converted to fat than refined sugars like sucrose and dextrose.

Carbohydrates are stored in the liver and muscles in the form of glycogen, which serves as the primary fuel source for muscle. Glycogen reservoirs are limited. It takes only about twenty minutes of moderate-intensity aerobic activity to deplete glycogen stores. Once they're gone, the body will dip into its fat stores.

Proteins

Proteins are the main building blocks of the body and, like carbohydrates, each gram contains four calories. Proteins are made up of complex chains of twenty different amino acids, twelve of which the body is able to manufacture. Because the human body lacks the necessary enzymes to synthesize the eight remaining amino acids from their components, these eight essential amino acids must be consumed in the diet. Active individuals typically require approximately one gram of protein per pound of ideal weight per day in order to maintain their lean tissue mass. Bodybuilders, strength athletes, and endurance athletes are in a perpetual cycle of muscle deconstruction and reconstruction and have even larger protein demands. Foods such as milk, cheese, eggs, poultry, red meat, and fish are rich sources of protein.

Fats

Contrary to popular belief, fats are not all bad, and are actually important energy sources when stored glycogen is limited. Fats contain nine calories per gram, more than twice the amount found in carbohydrates and proteins. Saturated fats, derived from animal sources, have been shown to contribute more heavily to the development of cardiovascular disease than unsaturated fats, derived from plant sources. For health reasons, fats should be limited to less than 20 percent of total consumed calories.

Alcohol

This is not exactly classified as a nutrient, but it is widely consumed and warrants mention. Alcohol is the enemy of the dieter and the athlete. It contains seven calories per gram, nearly as much as fat, and is completely without nutritional value. Not only does alcohol contribute empty calories, it slows the body's metabolic rate so that fewer calories are burned over time. In addition, alcohol consumption leads to a transient hypoglycemic state and subsequent food cravings. Finally, alcohol is hepatotoxic and even moderate drinking leads to fatty deposits on the liver. While the liver works hard to detoxify the system of alcohol, it is less efficient at lipolysis (fat burning).

General Dietary Guidelines

Eat frequent, small meals and be aware of the nutritional content of your food. Use a book or other guide to keep track of calories, protein, and fat. You should measure your food (with a measuring cup or scale) until you have a good idea of exactly what a "portion" actually represents. Most people grossly overestimate portion size and hence grossly underestimate their caloric intake.

For the best results in terms of high energy level, diminished body fat, muscle growth, and good gastrointestinal health, you should be eating five to six 200- to 300-calorie meals per day. Each meal should contain roughly the same amount of protein and carbohydrates with as little fat as possible. Better yet, limit starchy carbs to the first three meals of the day and have only fresh fruits and vegetables with the last three meals of the day.

No time to eat right five times a day? How long does it take to prepare a bag of turkey jerky and an apple? You should carry a supply of foods like these, which are high in protein and low glycemic index carbs, with you at all times. Keep a stash in you car, office, or gym bag. The longer you make your body wait between meals, the less efficient it becomes at burning fat, and the greater your chance of overeating when you finally allow yourself to have a meal.

One final piece of advice: be patient. Most people are frustrated by the difficulty they encounter losing those last few pounds of fat. You will achieve a lean, toned physique if you stick to the basic principles outlined in this chapter, train consistently, and give yourself time.

This material originally appeared in the July 1999 issue of Martial Arts Illustrated.

Protein Power
Why I'm Pro-Protein

Christine Lydon, M.D.

The structural integrity of virtually every tissue of the human body, including tendons, ligaments, muscles, and organs, relies on a protein framework. To maintain, rebuild, or add to existing muscle mass, the body must synthesize genetically defined protein configurations.

All proteins are complex molecular chains comprising different combinations of twenty amino acids, twelve of which the body is able to manufacture. The other eight essential ones must be consumed in the diet because the human body lacks the necessary enzymes to assemble them. During times of duress, such as surgery, illness, intensive training, or emotional upheaval, the body requires additional amounts of three particular amino acids.

These three, *L-arginine*, *L-glutamine*, and *L-histidine*, are referred to as *conditionally essential*. Nitrogen, which is integral to protein synthesis, is not found in fats or carbohydrates but is derived solely from protein sources. Proteins consumed in the diet are first broken down to smaller components by enzymes known as *proteases*, which are produced by the stomach, pancreas, and intestines. These smaller protein components are made up of varying numbers of amino acids.

When two or more amino acids are bound together chemically, they are called *peptides*. A *dipeptide* is comprised of two amino acids, a *tripeptide* contains three, and anything larger is referred to as an *oligopeptide*. Individual amino acids as well as small peptides are absorbed into the bloodstream through the intestinal lining. Once in the circulation, the amino acids are taken up by cells of various tissues where they are either used to synthesize new proteins, or deaminated and converted to glucose for energy.

Metabolism of amino acids is guided by the body's needs. When caloric and protein intake is adequate, amino acids are immediately used for growth and maintenance of tissues and the body is said to be in a state of *positive nitrogen balance*, a necessary prerequisite for muscle growth. When caloric intake falls short of the body's requirements, amino acids undergo a process known as *deamination*, whereby their nitrogen group is removed, incorporated into urea, and excreted by the kidneys. The remainder of the amino molecule is converted to glucose and used as an energy source.

Protein breakdown, or *catabolism*, begins with *branched chain amino acids (BCAAs)* whose unique side chain configuration facilitates their conversion to glucose. Since one-third of muscle tissue is comprised of BCAAs, muscle catabolism is an unavoidable consequence of inadequate dietary protein. In fact, up to 10 percent of calories consumed during exercise originate from the conversion of BCAAs to glucose. Studies demonstrate that BCAA supplementation not only enhances performance by improving endurance, but also permits muscle recovery during intense training.

It is impossible to overemphasize the importance of adequate dietary protein, especially for athletes. Both strength and endurance athletes exist in a perpetual cycle of muscle deconstruction and reconstruction and, as a result, have significantly greater protein requirements than nonathletes. Regardless of the sport, rigorous exercise results in microtears within muscle tissue. Contact sports and weight training lead to especially large degrees of muscular breakdown. Lacking sufficient protein intake, these tissues will neither develop fully nor recover rapidly. Beyond the obvious aesthetic, athletic, and health benefits of maximizing lean tissue retention, bear in mind that muscle is extremely metabolically active.

Maintaining lean tissue necessitates enormous caloric expenditure even when you're just sitting around doing nothing. Adipose tissue (fat), on the other hand, requires virtually no energy investment to survive. In essence, the more lean muscle tissue you possess, the more fat you will burn—regardless of your activity level!

Currently, the suggested daily requirement for protein consumption falls somewhere around 0.8 grams of protein per kilogram, or less than 0.4 grams of protein per pound of ideal body weight. Unfortunately, these recommendations were based on forty-year-old studies of sedentary individuals. More recent work by Peter Leman, PhD, of Kent State University indicates that endurance athletes should consume 1.2 to 1.4 grams of protein per kilogram of ideal body weight per day (0.6 grams per pound), and strength athletes (the study specified bodybuilders) are advised to consume 1.4 to 1.8 grams of protein per kilogram per day (0.6 to 0.8 grams per pound).

Although the scientific community is finally substantiating experimentally what bodybuilders have known empirically for years, my own experience has taught me that even Dr. Leman's revised recommendations are probably inadequate for many athletes. The "bodybuilders" that Dr. Leman used for his experiments included previously sedentary individuals who were subsequently placed on a workout program. None of his studies included competitive bodybuilders (or other strength-trained athletes) whose lean muscle mass would far exceed that of his study subjects.

My own recommendation for any individual who engages in intensive strength training at least three times a week is to consume a gram of protein per pound of lean body mass. I don't advise using "ideal" body weight as your guide since very muscular individuals invariably surpass their "weight chart" weight.

But how much protein do foods contain? A complete review of dietary protein sources exceeds the scope of this chapter, but a number of books are available that detail this information. Merely consuming adequate amounts of protein is not enough. Because the body is unable to store excess protein, it must be ingested every two to three hours to maximize lean tissue development and promote lipolysis (fat burning). For example, a 180-pound athletic man with 12 percent body fat has a lean body mass of 158 pounds and should consume roughly 160 grams of protein per day.

$$100\% - 12\% = 88\% \text{ lean tissue}$$
$$180 \text{ pounds} \times 88\% = 158 \text{ pounds}$$

He might eat a breakfast including six egg whites (20 grams), followed by a midmorning meal of a three-ounce chicken breast ($20 + 20 = 40$ grams), a lunch comprising one can of white meat tuna ($40 + 40 = 80$ grams), three ounces of turkey cold cuts for an afternoon snack ($80 + 20 = 100$), and a dinner including six ounces of flank steak ($100 + 60 = 160$).

Sound like a lot of work? Many active individuals have difficulty ingesting adequate dietary protein with sufficient frequency and opt to supplement with a quality protein powder.

What makes a protein supplement a quality product? First, it should be low in carbohydrates and fat. Second, it should have a superior amino acid profile. And last, it should have a high biological value (BV). BV measures the ability of food protein sources to deposit nitrogen into muscle tissue. Because there are numerous other nitrogen-containing compounds essential to human life (including DNA, RNA, heme, creatine, hormones such as thyroxine and epinephrine, pigments such as melanin, and so on), not all of the nitrogen retained by the body is used to manufacture protein. Hence, BV reflects both digestibility and efficiency of protein utilization.

If you are concerned about potential health risks associated with increased protein intake, rest assured that medical literature reveals no evidence that normal, healthy individuals experience health problems on high-protein diets. However, increased protein consumption should be accompanied by additional water intake because the excretion of nitrogen wastes results in higher urine output. I advise all active individuals to drink at least a gallon of fluids every day to ensure optimum kidney function, cleanse the system of toxins, and increase lipolysis.

If you do not think you have been consuming adequate protein up to this point, make a conscious effort to do so now, and I guarantee you will see and feel results within a couple of weeks. Your muscles will appear harder and fuller. You will feel stronger. You will notice decreased muscle soreness and will be more rested after the same recovery time. You will probably observe a decrease in body fat and increase in lean muscle mass. Only with adequate protein can you hope to reap the full benefits of your training and maximize your potential.

This material originally appeared in the September 1999 issue of Martial Arts Illustrated.

How Healthy People
Stay Healthy

Ray Sahelian, M.D.

Having treated thousands of patients for more than a decade, I have determined some of the reasons why some patients remain healthy and age slowly while others have a rapid deterioration of their physical and mental health. Although genetics plays a role in how we age, we cannot discount the significance of diet and lifestyle habits.

People who stay healthy and age gracefully maintain moderate eating habits with a good balance of protein, fat, and carbohydrate. Most of their carbohydrate comes from complex sources such as whole grains, soy, and other legumes. They include a few servings of a variety of fruits and vegetables each day. Most eat fish at least once or twice a week. Their intake of fried foods, fast foods, margarine, and baked goods is minimal.

Although refined foods, sweets, pastries, ice cream, and other high-sugar and high-fat foods are unhealthy, their complete avoidance is not necessary.

Most of us have a sweet tooth, and it's okay to occasionally indulge and satisfy the craving as long as the rest of the diet is healthy.

Varying one's food intake is crucial to obtaining the variety of nutrients, vitamins, and plant chemicals our bodies require. Attempt to consume citrus fruits, berries, apricots, grapes, and other colored fruits on a regular basis. Your vegetable intake should include garlic, onions, green leafy vegetables, yellow- or orange-colored vegetables, tomatoes, beets, and others.

Nothing seems to improve memory, mood, and overall mental health as much as regular, deep sleep. I recommend that patients expose themselves to morning light for at least ten to twenty minutes by either taking a walk or driving to work. Morning light exposure helps reset one's daily clock. Mental activity should be stopped at least one hour before bed and the mind allowed to switch to fun reading, or watching a comedy film or TV show. You could tape your favorite prime-time sitcom and then watch it before bed.

As a rule, I find patients who take appropriate supplements are less prone to infections or illness. One's supplement list does not need to take up multiple pages. I recommend to most patients to include at least one or two times the RDA for vitamins, and at least 50 percent of the RDA for minerals. In addition, I think it's beneficial to take between 100 and 300 mg of vitamin C, and 20 to 50 units of vitamin E. Vegetarians may need to supplement with a few additional nutrients that are mostly found in meats. For instance, CoQ_{10}, carnitine, and creatine are found only in small amounts in vegetarian diets. Hence, it would be appropriate to supplement with 10 to 30 mg of CoQ_{10}, 100 to 250 mg of carnitine, and one gram of creatine most days. Those whose fish intake is low would do well supplementing with fish oil capsules that contain at least 500 mg of the fatty acids EPA and DHA.

Life is always challenging us with obstacles. There can be deaths in the family, sickness, financial crises, and relationship problems. People who maintain their health throughout difficult periods have learned to become resilient. They do everything they can to minimize any problems or obstacles, but realize that sometimes these will occur despite our best efforts.

Hence, resiliency and proper attitude become key survival factors. Healthy people avoid being excessively angry, spiteful, jealous, or bitter. Just as the stock market is on a continual rise, with occasional dips and recessions, our lives can be seen the same way. We should try to maintain our balance through the bear markets.

As the well-known manuscript *Desiderata* says, "Go placidly amid the noise and haste and remember what peace there may be in silence."

This material originally appeared in the April 1999 issue of Inside Kung-Fu.

PART 6

Technique Training for Striking, Kicking, and Grappling

Wing Chun Meets *JKD*

Wooden Dummy Comparison

Tim Tackett

Bruce Lee spent a lot of time working on the dummy. Even though Bruce had not learned the entire *wing chun* dummy set, he was creative enough to freelance it using elements of the *wing chun* he had learned in Hong Kong plus boxing and other techniques. Former students such as Pete Jacobs, who saw Bruce working out on the dummy, have told me he hit it so hard it was frightening.

Working with the *wing chun* dummy is excellent supplemental training for *Jun Fan Jeet Kune Do* as well as an essential part of *wing chun* training. How should you accomplish this? If you don't have a person who can show you the proper way to use the dummy, experiment with any technique. Then absorb what is useful. Reject what is useless and add what is specifically your own. If you are a *Jun Fan Jeet Kune Do* practitioner you can make up a set pattern or patterns, but you must eventually dissolve these patterns and work in a more free-flowing, fashion.

This process is a lot easier if you are fortunate enough, as I was, to have an instructor such as Dan Inosanto. I started studying *JKD* with *Sifu* Inosanto shortly after Bruce Lee closed the Los Angeles Chinatown school, and many of Bruce's and Danny's advanced students started working out on Tuesday and Thursday evenings in *Sifu* Inosanto's backyard.

After Bruce Lee's tragic and untimely death, Inosanto went to Hong Kong to film the revised version of *The Game of Death*. While in Hong Kong Dan learned the complete *wing chun mook jong* form, which is comprised of 108 techniques divided into ten series, from a *wing chun* practitioner named Chris Yik. Dan taught many of his backyard *JKD* students the entire *wing chun* dummy set. Dan Inosanto then created a *Jeet Kune Do* dummy set consisting of Bruce Lee's modified *wing chun* techniques and the boxing phase of *JKD*.

It is clear from Bruce's notes that *JKD* is not based on twenty-six different martial arts, as has been reported. Bruce wrote that he had created a new martial art—*Jeet Kune Do*, or the way of the intercepting fist—based mainly on *wing chun*, Western boxing, and Western fencing. The *JKD* dummy set Dan created consists of 125 movements, most coming from Western boxing and modified *wing chun*.

This chapter will show you series one of the *wing chun* set and the first techniques of the *JKD* dummy set. While neither set is part of the core curriculum of *Jun Fan Jeet Kune Do*, it can be a valuable asset to the *Jun Fan Jeet Kune Do* practitioner. He can pick and choose from each form. He can learn the forms, then dissolve the forms so he can truly express himself.

Series 1: The *Wing Chun* Dummy Set

1. Face the dummy in a *wing chun* stance, right hand forward.

2. Wedge: Shove both hands forward hard between the dummy arms.

3. Palm hit

4. Inside lop with neck pull. Your left hand grabs the inside of the right dummy arm as your right hand pulls the dummy toward you.

5. *Bong sau*: *Bong sau* block to inside right dummy arm.

6. *Tan sau* with low palm hit: Step out with right leg and do a *tan* block while simultaneously hitting the dummy with your left palm.

7. *Guong sau*: Simultaneously perform a high parry and low block as you sweep the dummy leg.

8. *Quan sau*: Step out with your right leg as you simultaneously perform a high and low block.

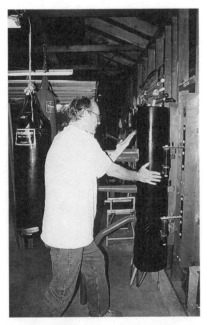

9. *Tan sau* with low palm hit: Same as previous *tan sau* move, but perform from the opposite side.

10. *Guong sau*: Same as previous *guong sau* move, but perform from the opposite side.

11. *Hyun sau*: Your right hand circles around the left dummy arm while you simultaneously block with your left arm.

12. Double *jyut sau*: Pull down with both wrists on both dummy arms.

13. Double palm hit: Bounce off the dummy arms with your jyut and hit the dummy with both palms.

14. *Tok sau*: End the first series with a double upward-palm block.

Series 2: The *Jeet Kune Do* Dummy Set

1. *By jong* ready position

2. Right step to the left with left outside parry.

3. Right step to the right with right outside parry.

4. Left step to the left with left high outside parry followed by . . .

5. Low right outside parry.

6. Right step to the right with right high outside parry, followed by . . .

7. Low left outside parry. (Note: 1–6 are passive moves and as such are the least desirable moves in *JFJKD*. It's all right to practice these if you realize that you are practicing parrying and that a simultaneous parry and hit is better. It is even better to hit and then parry.)

8. Step left with a left high outside parry and simultaneous right low punch.

9. Step right with a right high outside parry and simultaneous left low punch.

Series 3: Self-Defense Example—
The *Wing Chun* Set

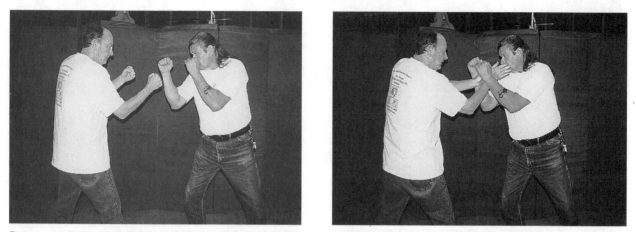

From a ready position (left), drive your hands with as much force as possible to open up his guard (right).

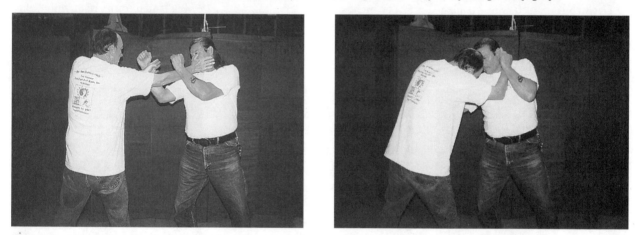

Hit his face with side palm (left). Grab his right wrist with your left (right), pull his neck, and headbutt.

Series 4: Self-Defense Example— The *JKD* Set

From a ready stance, your opponent throws a straight right lead (right).

Step left with your front foot with a high outside parry and follow with a straight lead punch to the face.

Tim Tackett is a founding member of the Jun Fan Jeet Kune Do Nucleus of the Jun Fan Jeet Kune Do Association. This material originally appeared in the February 1998 issue of Inside Kung-Fu.

Ring Around Your Opponent
Basic Principles and Strategies of the Ring

June Castro

Training for many years in several different martial arts, I have found the art of boxing to be the most underrated art with regard to self-defense, finesse, skill, technique, and strategies.

I've had conversations with martial artists who completely underestimate the martial intent of a well-trained boxer. My response is always the same: "It's quite obvious you've never stepped into the ring with a boxer, have you?"

The complexity of boxing goes beyond theory. It systematizes facts, principles, and training methods. Achieving proficiency is derived from observation, study, training, and conditioning. Learning the art of boxing begins with floor work. Here a student learns proper footwork, distance, balance, and leverage. The student is also taught the five basic punches: *jab*, *cross*, *hook*, *uppercut*, and *overhand*. Next, shadowboxing allows a student to incorporate these elements in a free-flowing manner.

Training on the various types of equipment is also important. Learning to hit focus mitts, heavy bags, speed bags, and double-end bags helps a fighter improve power, quickness, timing, and distance. While floor work and equipment training are invaluable to a fighter's training regimen, it's only the beginning. The fighter now must take his training to "the ring."

Fools Rush In

I had trained in the art of boxing for several years before actually learning the importance of ring training. It wasn't until I met and began training with my current coach, Garth Redwood, that I began to understand strategies and principles of the ring. While there are great fighters and great trainers, rarely is there a person who is endowed with equal

From a starting position (left), June executes a jab and Garth Redwood parries the punch with his rear hand (right).

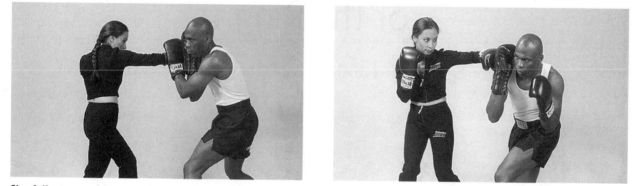

She follows up with a cross and he parries with the lead hand (left). She then lands a lead hook (right).

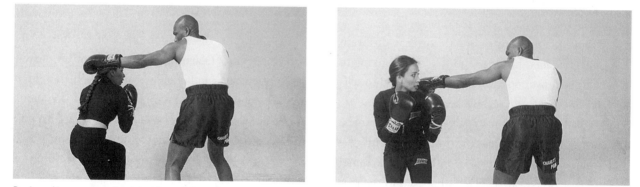

Redwood returns a lead hook and June bobs to the inside (left). She then weaves to the outside (right).

June returns a cross (left) and follows with a lead uppercut (right).

talents. Jamaican-born "Redwood," as he is affectionately referred to by his friends and students, is the rare exception.

Growing up in New York, Redwood was a troubled youth who rose from adversity and found discipline and honor through the martial arts. He is a fifth-degree black belt in karate, a former kickboxing champion, and a professional boxer. His first coach was the famed Bill Slayton, former trainer of boxing great Ken Norton. Redwood was also coached by the well-known Don Familton, and although there are many fighters who have the good fortune of training with excellent coaches, Redwood has a unique talent and an uncanny understanding of the intricacies of boxing.

When I first began training with Redwood, I looked at the ring as boundary lines and a novelty of boxing, and not as an integral part of training. "When a fighter steps into the ring to face his opponent, he must command the ring. There are specific principles and strategies a fighter must thoroughly understand if he intends to dominate and win the fight," says Redwood. The four elements of ring strategies include the *perimeter*, the *center*, the *ropes*, and the *corner*. The following are basic principles, concepts, and training drills taught by Redwood that give fighters a working knowledge of the ring.

The Perimeter

The perimeter is the distance from the ropes to the center of the ring. In general, this is where most fights begin. In the perimeter of the ring, your opponent's fighting style can be immediately determined. A fighter who is one dimensional is very predictable, because she favors moving forward and to only one side. The alternative is a difficult person to fight, because the opponent is very comfortable moving laterally as well as forward and back.

During the first minute of the round you must study your opponent's movement and footwork to find out whether she prefers moving to a particular side. To determine which direction your opponent

prefers to move, step in with the jab. After initiating the jab, move to the left or the right. This will force your opponent to react. If she stumbles, moves flat-footed, or glances down at her feet, you know which side is her weakness. However, if your opponent moves equally well to both sides, you know you are in for a tough fight. After stepping in with the jab and moving to either side, avoid leaning your head forward, keep your weight under you, and be ready to counter.

Within the perimeter you can be pursued, or you can draw your opponent to you. If you are being pursued, you will discover whether your opponent chases you down, or cuts your angles. If she simply chases you down, you can set her up, throw a combination, and quickly step out of range. If she's a heavy hitter, you must stick and move. For obvious reasons, you never want to go toe-to-toe with a fighter who is stronger than you are. Also, when dealing with a heavy hitter, knowing how to tie her up will allow you to offset her distance.

If a fighter knows how to advance by cutting your angles, she is a difficult opponent. By cutting your angle when moving forward, your opponent restricts your space, thus making it difficult for you to maneuver and to execute combinations. If this is the case, you must adjust your position to the center of the ring.

Draw your opponent to you by hitting and moving. Stepping in with the jab, and then retreating back or to the side, will lure your opponent to you. Drawing is especially effective against an aggressive fighter who advances straight forward and does not understand the technical aspect of angling.

The Center

In the ring you must know how to work the center to your best advantage. The center of the ring is where a boxer has room to maneuver. It is critical for a fighter to understand how to utilize his capabilities within this area. Offensively a fighter can dance around his opponent to unleash a barrage of

From a starting position . . .

. . . the combination begins with a jab (left) and a cross (right).

Redwood returns a lead hook to the body (left) and June drops to shield with her forearm, which positions her to counter with a cross (right).

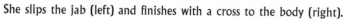

She slips the jab (left) and finishes with a cross to the body (right).

combinations. Defensively he can slip, bob, weave, and pivot around the opponent to not only make him miss, but to tire him out as well. Working the center is all about movement and strategies.

The Ropes

"The ropes can be your best friend or your worst enemy," states Redwood. Knowing how to use the ropes is an advantage only if you understand the basic principles. If you think the ropes are simply the boundaries of the ring, you will find yourself in a world of trouble. Getting backed up against the ropes and not understanding basic defensive maneuvers can be detrimental to a fighter. Offensively the ropes can be used to tie up your opponent (not in the literal sense), or draw him to you. Defensively, you can pivot to the side and follow up with combinations, or spin off the ropes to put your opponent at the disadvantage.

If you are being backed into the ropes, it is vital that you understand positioning. When moving back, you must shift your weight forward and retreat with the back leg to feel for the bottom rope. After making contact with the rope you have two options. The first is to pivot to the side, and follow through with combinations. The second is to brace for contact, then pivot to the side and follow up. Leaning your back up against the ropes is not an option, because it puts you in a vulnerable position.

Now on the other hand, if you are the aggressor, it is very important you do not follow the opponent in. If you do so, your opponent can pivot to the side and overwhelm you with combinations. Instead, stop short and feint or throw a punch to make him commit to moving to either side.

Then step to that side and follow up with an appropriate combination. If your opponent reacts with a punch, counter and follow through. Great fighters such as Roy Jones Jr. and Azuma Nelson know how to use the ropes to their advantage. For a magnificent display of manipulating an opponent on the ropes, watch the man who invented the "Rope a Dope," Muhammad Ali.

The Corner

The advantage of trapping your opponent in the corner helps you unleash a multitude of combinations. To direct your opponent to this ideal position, cut her angle of movement. If she moves to the left, you move to the right. If she steps to the right, then move to the left. By stepping to the opposite side, and angling forward, you can manipulate the direction in which your opponent moves.

If you end up in the corner, you must continue moving by shifting from side to side. Standing in one position is dangerous, because you become an easy target. It is also important that you know how to cover up and protect yourself. Although caught in the corner is not an optimal position, there are several options. You can brace for contact, you can counter an attack, you can tie the opponent up, you can pivot to the side, or you can reverse the position by spinning out and pushing the opponent into the corner. Once the tables have been turned you can follow up with a combination series.

Understanding basic principles and strategies of the ring is an essential part of a boxer's training program. The fight game is a tough business, so your training must prepare you to handle infinitely variable situations. Proper ring training from a competent coach will make the difference between having the confidence to command the ring and dictating the fight to charging forward and hoping for a knockout.

Expecting to rush in and knock out your opponent is foolish and dangerous. Be an intelligent fighter. Boxing is a science, so study hard, train well, and stay safe.

This material originally appeared in the August 1998 issue of Inside Kung-Fu.

26

Hands Like Stone in 100 Days

James W. McNeil

The martial arts demonstration is almost over, with one final event remaining—the iron hand. Two black belt students place a stack of twenty tiles next to a pile of nine bricks. No spacers are used. The boisterous crowd falls silent as an old man walks onto the stage and places himself before the stack of tiles. He looks at them for a moment, closes his eyes, and breathes deeply. Then, with a powerful thrust of his fist, he breaks them all.

Next, he places himself before the bricks, and again takes a moment to focus. Then, with a slap of the hand, he breaks all nine, demonstrating the awesome and devastating power of an iron palm blow.

(*Editor's note*: The iron hand training techniques mentioned in this article must always be done under the supervision of a qualified instructor. Do not try these methods on your own.)

A major aspect of mastery in any external martial art is the toughening of bones, skin, and muscles. Board and brick breaking is the traditional method of demonstrating this physical and mental toughness. While many martial arts styles have developed unique techniques for hardening the body, they can all be traced back to the *Shaolin* temples and their iron hand training methods.

What Is Iron Hand?

Many of us have heard of the legendary iron hand, but what is it and how is it attained? The term *iron hand* refers to a properly developed human hand that becomes hard like iron and generates tremendous power.

It is not known exactly from whom or in what dynasty the art originates, though it is believed to be from the Taoist and *Shaolin* temples of China. The only difference between the iron fist of *karate* and iron hand of *kung fu* is the priority of striking surfaces. As their names imply, iron fist prefers hitting with the knuckles, whereas iron hand strikes with all parts of the hand.

Mastering iron hand takes about two years, but you can see great improvement in only 100 days. It is essential before you begin this training to make sure you have a qualified teacher, one who has undergone and mastered the different methods involved in iron hand training. A good teacher should also be like a physician, with extensive knowledge of herbs, bone setting, massage, and other healing modalities. Even in today's world, the teacher should earn a reputation as a healer. Many claim to be masters of the iron hand, yet remain mere novices as they themselves have never had a true teacher.

Once a suitable teacher has been found, a student must adhere to these four very important, basic principles:

- *Trust*—and do exactly as your teacher instructs
- *Determination*—practice diligently and finish what you start
- *Endurance*—practice hard and be prepared to make sacrifices
- *Patience*—don't be in a hurry to achieve goals (such as breaking bricks) too soon; your teacher will know when you are ready

You should not begin the iron hand training until you learn patience; your hand cannot be conditioned overnight! Meditation and *chi kung* exercises will help you achieve this. There are some iron hand techniques that are closely guarded secrets shown only to those involved in actual training. A student should be of superior moral character.

Throughout the duration of training, one must always use *dit da jow* or iron hand liniment. This will keep the hands from becoming disfigured; the impact of continuously striking hard surfaces makes the blood stagnate, which in turn affects the vital organs and causes the hands to become permanently callused. This liniment is made in the traditional way by combining Chinese herbs with alcohol or vinegar and then letting the mixture steep for a period of years.

Get the Message?

At the beginning and end of each training session the liniment must be massaged or soaked deeply into the skin to enhance circulation and prevent bruising and internal injuries. The Taoists believe in preserving the hands, not destroying them. If the liniment is not used, the risk of internal hemorrhaging and even death is great. Many practitioners have ruined their hands for life by neglecting to use the liniment on a consistent basis.

Iron hand training is divided into three parts: *strengthening the hand*, *breathing*, and *methods of striking*. The most important phase of training is in learning how, where, and when to strike. To this end, extensive study of the human anatomy and physiology is undertaken. Different charts are used to examine the placement and interrelationships of the tendons, ligaments, muscles, bones, and internal organs. Most important, perhaps, is the study of the circulation of the blood and its position in the body at any given time during a twenty-four-hour cycle.

The blood has a cell that acts as "leader" of all the cells in the blood. This cell "leads" the blood, which is influenced by the sun and the moon, around the body. Knowing the exact location of this cell is imperative because this is where the blow must be directed when it is desired to kill or disable an opponent.

To kill an opponent, all the energy stored in the hand must be released. By releasing only part of the energy, instantaneous death is avoided. In some systems, "three" is used for delayed death timing: According to the amount of energy released, the opponent is given three hours, three days, or three weeks to live. This "delayed death touch" is used to give the opponent a chance to mend his ways. When a person is struck by an iron palm blow, a burning sensation is followed by the forming of blisters. As long as the blisters remain on the surface of the skin, death will not occur. However, if the blow were to penetrate deeply to a cellular level (to the "leader" cell in the blood), death would be inevitable.

Reviving and restoring the health of the recipient of an iron palm blow requires special study. A specific medicine that restores energy to the injured cell must also be taken.

Several different methods are used in iron hand training.

First Method

Stand in water up to your thighs and strike into it every day until your shoulders get very sore. When hitting the water you should try to make it splash up to form an open flower. This method sounds simple, but it is difficult to master.

Second Method

Fill a pan approximately two feet in diameter with a mixture of Chinese herbs, sand, and pebbles, and place it over a low fire. Then, standing in front of the pan, use a combination of striking, mixing, and grabbing with your bare hands for about an hour. During this time the herb, sand, and pebble mixture heats up. The temperature can vary from lukewarm to as hot as you can stand. The higher the temperature, the faster you move your hand while stirring or striking. After your hands have been "cooked," you must soak them in another type of medicine. The cooking is done to store the energy and heat of the fire in the hands, in the same way a battery stores electricity. Later, the cooking is not necessary since the student can retain energy in the hand by proper breathing and concentration of *chi*.

Third Method

This method is similar to the second method. The hands are cooked in Chinese herbs, but without the sand and pebbles, for about twenty minutes. Special breathing techniques are done while stirring the liquid. After cooking the hands, which heals any damage and prevents blood clots from forming, the

Jonus soaking his hand in hot herbs while doing a special breathing exercise.

student repeatedly thrusts his hands into a drum filled with beans—and, later, round iron pellets. The hands must be cooked in the herbs before and after each training session. To master it, this training should last about two years. With both the second and the third method the teacher must check his student to make sure he has not lost any sensitivity in his hand.

Fourth Method

This is the "slapping method," in which one can see great results in only 100 days. With a relaxed, easy motion, slap a bag filled with beans. The whole hand must be used: the palm, the ridge, the back, the edge, and the fist. Starting with 50 hits, the number of repetitions is gradually increased—50 strikes the first week, 75 the second, and 100 the third. The training should be practiced for 100 days, morning and evening.

Jeff hitting the bag with the knife edge of his hand

Fifth Method

This method requires hitting the back of the hand with a special tool, being careful not to injure the hand, to strengthen the back of the hand. This training can cause great damage if not correctly taught by a qualified teacher who has completed this training. You should do this training for three months. After mastering this method, you can easily drive a spike into a piece of wood with the back of the hand.

Scott pounding a spike with the back of his hand

Sixth Method

To develop a quick, snapping slap or backfist, practice by throwing stones with a backhand slapping motion. Throw the stones as hard as you can, and don't worry about accuracy. Working in this way every day for one year will strengthen and energize your hand.

Exercises for Grip Strength

A powerful grip complements and enhances iron hand training. Several exercises improve grip strength, including simple pushups. Do them on the knuckles and the fingertips, starting with five fingers and gradually decreasing to one. Another good drill is to hang from a tree limb and swing for as long as you can. If you don't have a tree available, you can hang from the top of a door. Another grip-strengthening exercise, one that is very traditional, is to fill a jar with sand and carry it around as long as you can. The jar's mouth should be narrow enough for you to grip with your fingertips, yet wide enough so that your hand is stretched. Increase the length of time, every day, then add more sand and start over.

Birgitta completing pushups on two fingers

Breathing Exercise

Before and after iron hand training it is necessary to do a breathing exercise that will put energy into the hands and make them stronger. A true iron hand practitioner or *chi kung* instructor should be able to put energy into any part of his body at will.

1. Stand with your feet about shoulder-width apart and inhale as you concentrate all your energy into your hands (remember, the mind guides the *chi*). Bring your hands up to your shoulders and then exhale as you compress all the energy into your hands as you push them forward. Do this three times.

2. Inhale as you concentrate all your energy into your hands. Bring your hands up to your shoulders and then exhale as you push your hands to the side. Do this three times.

3. Inhale as you continue to concentrate all your energy into your hands and push downward. Do this three times.

Advanced levels of iron hand training entail learning how to penetrate the skin of a human or animal. A large barrel is used with a skin stretched across the top. Inside is a tomato or other soft fruit. The practitioner must penetrate the skin and grab the tomato without damaging the fruit. He must be solid, then soft, all with lightning speed.

An authentic iron hand master does not need to resort to tricks when performing demonstrations. His skill should speak for itself. Next time you witness a demonstration, consider the following:

- Are spacers being used between slabs? The use of spacers will make breaking a stack of bricks, tiles, or ice considerably easier; the first slab will break the second and so on.
- A large slab may look impressive, but is actually much easier to break than a smaller, more compact version.
- Breaking a coconut can be very difficult, unless you hit it on the seam.
- A sheet of ice will shatter on impact. If it makes a clean break, you will know that it was precut.

Like anything worthwhile, mastering these iron hand techniques will come only through intense hard work and dedication to training. But if you are willing to pay the price, the rewards will be beyond your wildest dreams.

Danny starts to raise his hands (left) during breathing exercises—he is putting energy into his hands. Danny raises his hands over his head (center) after completing the inhalation. He then pushes his hands outward (right) as he compacts the *chi* in his hands while exhaling.

Larry thrusts through the leather-covered drum.

Dagmar breaks a coconut with her hand.

Sifu James McNeil breaking twenty tiles with his fist (without spacers)

Sifu James McNeil offers iron hand training at his Little Nine Heaven Taoist Institute in Rainbow, California. He teaches it as he was taught by Master Ralph Shun (southern style shaolin), Master C. Y. Chin (poison fingers), Master Chou Chang Hung (Little Nine Heaven Kung Fu and paqua), and Master Hsu Hong Chi (Hsing I and eagle claw) in Taiwan. This material originally appeared in the July 1998 issue of Inside Kung-Fu.

27

Muay Thai Training Techniques

Drosos Michalis with Mark Komuro

A class from the Atlas Gym practices *Muay Thai.*

Greece. The Olympics. Mythological gods. *Muay Thai?* Today, *Muay Thai* is quickly gaining popularity as a major martial art in Thailand.

The first time I saw *Muay Thai* was in France. I was amazed by the way the two Thai guys were fighting. It was unlike anything I had seen or experienced before. It looked like kickboxing, but participants were also using knees and elbows and were fighting from the clinch. I knew I had to learn more about this sport.

I stayed in Thailand for two months and trained daily. Although my twenty years of kickboxing helped me adjust to the rhythm of *Muay Thai*, I marveled at the technique the Thais exhibited. Everything was like second nature to them. *Muay Thai* was

Training in the focus mitts gives the fighter the chance to coordinate hand and eye movement and build hand speed.

more powerful and gives them the self-confidence they have been lacking. My students find the training realistic and are attracted by the unique Thai culture. Special children's classes with kids as young as eight lay a good foundation for the school.

Muay Thai training is one of the most demanding of any sport. At the Atlas Gym the fighting class

in their blood. Because of our language differences, no one could explain *Muay Thai* to me. When I left Thailand I began my search for more knowledge about the art. Every little detail gave me new energy to do more.

Finding the Right Teacher

Finally, I read about Kru Vut Kamnark in a magazine. I wrote to him and, after much correspondence, flew to the United States to train. I found not only an instructor, but also a close friend.

My gym in Greece—the Atlas Gym—is not very big, but it has all a fighter could ask for. All the equipment is top quality. But what is more important, every member of the gym feels like a part of a family that numbers more than one hundred. Classes consist of *karate*, kickboxing, and self-defense, but both old and new students are most interested in learning *Muay Thai*. They tell me it is because it's

The heavy bag is an essential element of the training necessary for building strength in a fighter.

Vut Kamnark (left) and Drosos Michalis work on sparring, one of the most important parts of *Muay Thai* training.

situps and pushups are done in sets of 100, followed by stretches to cool down the body.

Muay Thai training remains new to those outside Asia, but the more people see its effectiveness as a tool for health and self-defense, the more it will gain popularity in the West.

This material originally appeared in the November 1998 issue of Inside Kung-Fu.

starts with three, three-minute rounds of jumping rope. Next comes shadowboxing for three more rounds, emphasizing proper form and speed. Next, four rounds of training on the heavy bag or Thai kicking pads build strength and endurance. Three more rounds on the top and bottom bag build hand speed and coordination.

The next step has each fighter partner up and practice techniques, including clinches, knees, and elbows. At this stage the technique is controlled, with the fighters more concerned with form and timing without going full force. The last stage is sparring with fighters matched up by size and skill. This allows the coach to analyze the fighters and helps the fighters practice and challenge their skills. Finally,

Much time is devoted to children because they represent future champions. Children begin practicing *Muay Thai* at age five, and many practice on a daily basis.

Muay Thai gives women the self-confidence they need to face any difficulty. That's one reason they prefer it to other sports.

Vut Kamnark barrels into his opponent during a training session.

28

The Grappler's Conditioning and Drilling Blueprint

Robert Ferguson

Much can be said about conditioning and drilling. After all, the martial artist who makes these two essentials part of her training will have the edge, for being proactive is being prepared.

To be properly prepared for competition and self-defense, you must be proactive and, therefore, in a state of readiness. It is not what you do days before a competition that prepares you to win, but what you do weeks and months prior to the event.

All too often you will meet a grappler who has respectable knowledge and skill and appears to be confident, yet once he begins to wrestle to submission, his inner adversary—fatigue—attacks. He runs out of gas because he has little or no endurance and cardiovascular training. For this reason alone, being proactive is important; being responsible and prepared for competition will determine your performance.

Let's take, for example, a grappler who practices techniques in preparation for competition—no running, sprinting, live sparring, or strength training, only technical proficiency. If she has to compete only once, if the match is less than one minute in length, and if the opponent only practices techniques, she may win. Nonetheless, in reality she may have to fight more than one opponent, the match may last five or six minutes, and the opponent may be in elite physical condition. If she doesn't properly prepare herself physically, fatigue will likely become a factor and the hundreds of techniques she is familiar with will remain unused, solely because she will not possess the physical resources to execute them. If you're unable to assume the proper competitive work ethic, you're in for a rude awakening.

Case in point. You don't wait until you get into an automobile accident before you purchase collision insurance. It is only wise to be responsible and

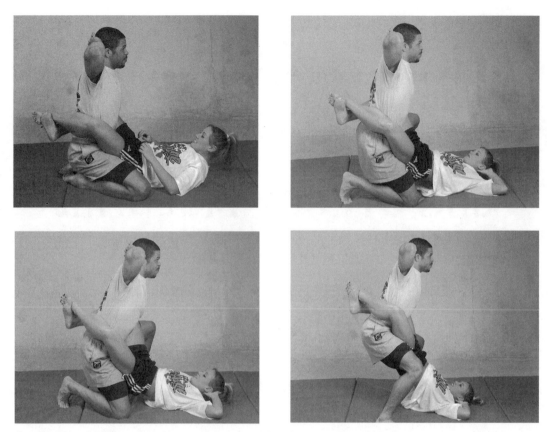

Conditioning drill: To strengthen your guard and legs for grappling, look no further. Michele Krasnoo attains a closed guard while Robert Ferguson assumes good posture. Both Krasnoo and Ferguson place their hands behind their heads. The objective in this drill is for Krasnoo to keep her legs crossed while Ferguson exercises his quadriceps and balance by standing up. After standing up, Ferguson slowly returns to the beginning position. Both Krasnoo and Ferguson will perform this conditioning drill ten times on each side.

properly prepared for what may likely happen. I've always said it is better to act than to react.

To take a proactive approach to training, you must explore your current muscular strength and endurance, cardiovascular efficiency, flexibility, grappling ability, and training methods. You must also evaluate your present eating habits. By initially taking action toward assessing your overall skills, athleticism, and lifestyle, you will be better equipped to excel in submission wrestling.

Eating Habits

We all have a pretty good idea of how to eat to be healthy, but good eating habits are easier to talk about

than to practice. Establishing a proper diet is much more difficult than maintaining one. Therefore, until you make your new eating habits permanent, it may prove beneficial for you to avoid spending time with, or at least eating with, the people in your life who are a negative influence on what you eat. If you are an alcoholic in pursuit of sobriety, you will not gain strength or stop drinking if you're spending time around others who drink.

Obviously, you must avoid sweets, foods high in fat and cholesterol, and soda if you want to be proactive toward preparing your body for competition. There are no secrets or cryptic eating formulas that make up the most nutritional diet. Simply keep in mind that if you want a healthy body, you must eat healthy food.

Power situps: When you engage in grappling you are guaranteed to properly condition your abdominal muscles, quadriceps, and hamstrings. This is the prime reason women are taking to the grappling arts—the fitness focus and essential self-defense skills. Begin the power situp, keeping your elbows out and hands behind your head. Continue by simply sitting up and then thrusting forward; finish in a standing position. Krasnoo performs three sets of twenty power situps.

Muscular Strength and Endurance

When two grapplers who are equal in technical prowess, cardiovascular conditioning, and athletic ability contend with each other, the deciding factor often comes down to strength. Many grapplers claim that technique and leverage determine the victor. I agree that in most instances, the better grappler has greater technical skill. However, when both grapplers are equally skilled and prepared, the stronger fighter has the advantage.

Weight lifting and calisthenics that improve your overall strength and endurance may be done with the guidance of an expert. Seek the advice and skill of professionals who work with athletes eager to increase strength and endurance for their specific sport or activity. An expert can be reached at practically every fitness gym and training center. Be wise and eager to attain the advice and guidance of those who make it a profession.

Muscular development can be divided into three categories: *Muscular endurance* is performing moderate- to low-level work for an extended period of time, such as a cycling race; *muscular strength* is generating maximal force irrespective of time, such as in distance rowing; and *muscular power* is generating the greatest force possible within a short period of time, such as sprinting. How you train for strength is based upon your desired strength goal. When wrestling to submission, you want a combination of all three qualities, with an emphasis on muscular strength.

Strength can also be subdivided into *pure strength* and what many grapplers refer to as *mat strength*. Pure strength refers to strength developed outside a sport or application context. Force generated during weight training is pure strength. Mat strength, or *speed strength*, is developed or transferred to grappling and applying submission techniques.

Submission wrestling is an example of mat strength, whereas weight lifting is usually considered pure strength. The little research done on the relationship between these two qualities indicates one should first build pure strength, then adapt that strength when sparring on the mat. A grappler should develop pure strength via resistance training, and then gradually begin to adapt that strength to submission wrestling by sparring. Resistance training should be a base before power is developed.

Cardiovascular Efficiency and Endurance

Run . . . run . . . run! Grapple . . . grapple . . . grapple! Distance running, sprints, and sparring on the mat are great for improving cardiovascular efficiency and endurance. However, it must be understood that not everyone can run, sprint, and grapple efficiently. Well, at least not in the beginning. If you fall into the category of not being able to run and sprint, consult with a fitness expert to design a program for you structured around your physical limits.

At the same time, implement training that combines high- and low-intensity intervals. Interval training will prove effective for both the aerobic and anaerobic systems. You will definitely maximize your cardiovascular efficiency and endurance via interval

training. Interval training will increase your ability to grapple with intensity for long periods of time.

The goal of interval training is to push both the aerobic and anaerobic systems to their limits. Alternating brief periods of high-intensity work with low-intensity recovery periods results in overloading both energy systems. During continuous exercise, oxygen is supplied to and used by the working muscles. Hence, there is a balance between oxygen available for the body's use and how it functions. You will quickly discover with submission wrestling how your aerobic and anaerobic systems can be exhausted simultaneously.

Flexibility

Flexibility is an important fitness component that many athletes want to improve. Theories on stretching and enhancing flexibility abound. Developing a healthy range of motion will allow you to stretch to a greater extent, keep your muscles supple, and better respond to the demands of daily activities and exercise.

Grapplers should stretch to improve flexibility on a daily basis. The benefits attributed to stretching are improved movement function, reduced muscle tension, enhanced relaxation, improved posture and coordination, reduced stiffness, and delay of physical deterioration associated with aging. Suppleness, or keeping your muscles loose and limber, is definitely an asset if excelling in submission wrestling and/or grappling is the goal.

Sport-Specific Drilling and Conditioning

Before participating in submission wrestling, it is important and highly recommended that you physically condition yourself and practice drills that

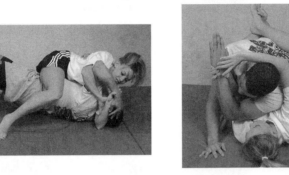

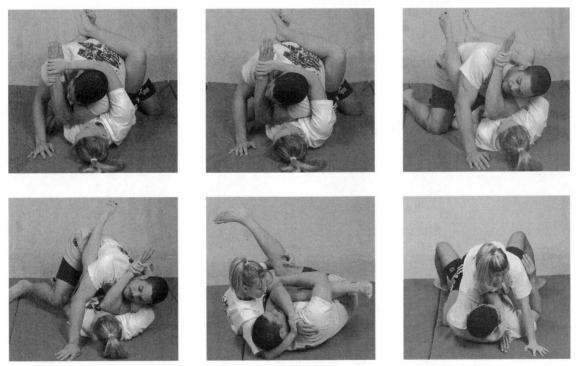

Submission-reversal drill: Krasnoo assumes the mounted position and applies a figure-four shoulder crank (first row). Once Ferguson taps, he then bridges and rolls Krasnoo to her back (second row, left). Once to her back, Krasnoo assumes a closed guard and traps Ferguson's arm (second row, right, and third row). Once the arm is trapped, Krasnoo continues the drill by dropping her right leg (fourth row, left) and hooking her left hand behind Ferguson's leg. At this time Krasnoo pushes her left leg into Ferguson's side, and in a sweeping fashion she reverses the situation (fourth row, middle) and assumes the mount (fourth row, right). At this time, Krasnoo repeats the sequence ten times on each side.

directly enhance your ability to perform. Besides, proper conditioning will improve performance, increase skill, and help to prevent the injuries most common in submission wrestling. Keep in mind, accidents occur most frequently when muscles tire and reflexes slow. Strong muscles won't tire as quickly, so you can spend more time grappling and less time recovering from strains and sprains.

Submission Wrestling's Physical Needs

There are similarities in practically all conditioning programs. However, each sport is unique, as is its training program. These differences must be recog-

nized and defined. As a grappler you must learn the physical demands of submission wrestling to improve your performance. If you are unfamiliar with submission wrestling and grappling, watch a class or event carefully to see what muscles are involved and how they move during an actual performance. This will give you valuable clues as to what exercises need special attention.

In submission wrestling, strength, flexibility, and endurance are vital. For this reason, you must design a specific training program that caters to the physical and technical demands that submission wrestling puts on your body. Meanwhile, you will develop your technical skill as well.

Although running will increase your overall performance when sparring, nothing is better than

Grappling situps: To begin, simply assume the position shown in the upper-left photo. Then, keeping your knees together, bring them toward your chest (upper right). Elevate your hips upward while keeping your feet lower than your knees (above, middle).

An application of the grappling situp

Here, Krasnoo demonstrates how you can get back to a standing position using the grappling situp. Krasnoo performs five sets of twenty grappling situps.

getting on the mat and engaging in situation grappling—improving technical skill. For instance, your training partner is mounted on top of you. He has the position of advantage, and your goal is to maneuver him into your guard while he makes every effort to maintain the mount. This type of training is specific in purpose, for it is likely you'll find yourself mounted and struggling to escape and reverse the situation.

Determining the components necessary to excel in submission wrestling is no easy task. However, once you examine the physical requirements of submission wrestling, you will discover the following components that need to be addressed: aerobic and anaerobic energy systems; muscular strength, power, and endurance, primarily for the neck, thighs, hips,

back, and abdomen; and flexibility for the total body. These following ten exercises are recommended in addition to situation grappling and wrestling to submission:

1. Pushups
2. Jumping rope
3. Squats
4. Wind sprints
5. Distance running
6. Jump squats
7. Situps
8. Standing lunges
9. Bend and thrusts
10. Buddy carries

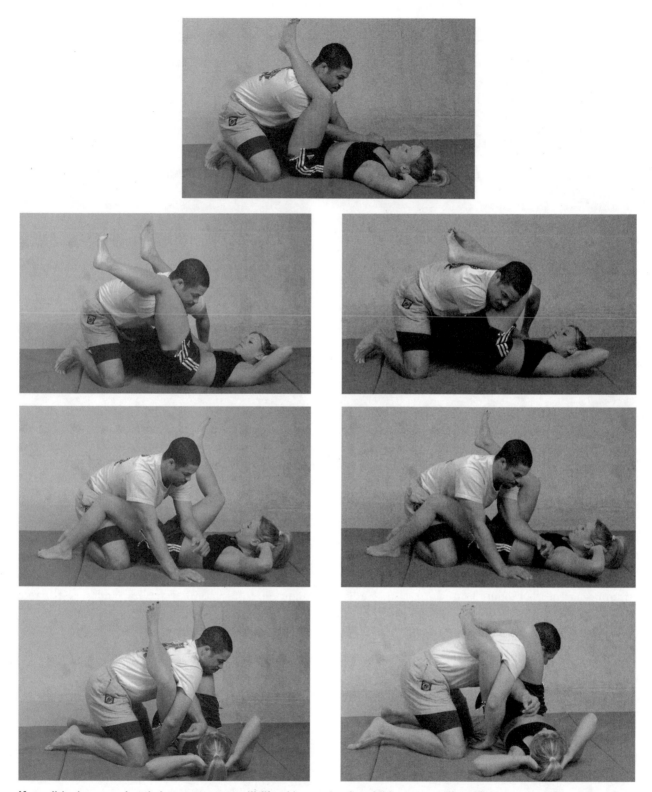

If conditioning your legs is important, you will like this exercise. In addition, you will condition your ability to arm bar your opponent from the guard. To begin, assume the closed guard (top photo). Ferguson places his right arm on Krasnoo's stomach (second row, left). She then places the back of her left knee atop Ferguson's left shoulder (second row, right). Krasnoo pushes her right leg into Ferguson's shoulder while moving her left leg toward his right shoulder, simultaneously causing her to rotate her hips (third row, left). Once Krasnoo positions herself to the side (third row, right), she squeezes her knees together and pulls her heels to her rear (fourth row, left). Krasnoo should be able to hold Ferguson's arm with her legs alone. Krasnoo repeats the same exercise to the opposite side (fourth row, right).

Last Words

Practically all sports and martial arts have training drills that heighten the competitors' ability and fundamental skills. Basketball players have drills that enhance dribbling, boxers use focus mitt drills that increase timing and accuracy, and *kung-fu* practitioners have trapping drills that expand their overall performance. Learning to drill via situation grappling and similar activity is simply disguising the mother of all skill—repetition.

This material originally appeared in the June 1999 issue of Inside Kung-Fu.

How Marco Ruas
Prepares for Competition

Norm Leff

He is tall, he is strong, he is muscular, and he looks like he can walk through walls. His name is Marco Ruas.

Ruas has a very impressive physique, and he will likely get bigger, stronger, and more muscular as long as he continues to fight. He stands six feet two inches in his bare feet and weighs in at about 230 pounds of pure muscle. The following is his very own detailed explanation of how he trains for a fight.

Training Routine

The length of time needed to prepare for a fight is two months. Ruas trains twice a day. In the morning, he begins with a stretching session for about ten minutes. After he finishes stretching, he works on his abdominal muscles. Here are the ten abdominal exercises that Ruas does six days per week. For each exercise, he does 1 set of 100 reps.

1. Crunches
2. Leg raises
3. Knee raises (knee lifts up to chest)
4. V-ups (half situp with the knees brought into the chest)
5. Jackknives (half situp with a leg raise; arms are extended while trying to touch the toes)
6. Alternate knees to the chest
7. Alternate leg raises
8. V-ups (left elbow touching the right knee, and the right elbow touching the left knee)
9. Jackknives (done in the same way as exercise eight—left elbow touches the right knee and the right elbow the left knee)
10. Twisting crunches

Road Work

Ruas usually runs for forty minutes without stopping, or he runs fast for two minutes then slows down the pace for a minute. He does this twenty times. He then swims for thirty minutes. After swimming, he rides on a stationary bicycle for another thirty minutes.

Weight Training

His weight-training exercises are usually done in the morning. He works out with weights three times per week. Each body part is generally trained once a week.

First Weight-Training Session

Exercise	Sets	Reps
CHEST		
Bench press with barbell	3	15
Parallel bar dips	3	15
SHOULDERS		
Bench press with barbell	3	15
Parallel bar dips	3	15
Standing lateral raises	3	15

Second Weight-Training Session

Exercise	Sets	Reps
BACK		
Pullups	3	15
Cable rows (seated)	3	15
LEGS		
Leg extensions	3	15
Leg curls	3	15
Leg presses	4	25
Calf raises	3	25
LOWER BACK		
Deadlift	3	15

Ruas trains with weights every other day, using moderate weights with high repetitions. On Monday he does the first session; on Wednesday he does the second session; on Friday he does the first again, then does the second again on Monday, and so on.

Ruas is very strong. He told me that he could bench press 440 pounds! His weight training is for strength, stamina, body conditioning, and endurance. The reason he does not do more weight training is because he is a fighter, not a bodybuilder.

Ruas mentioned that it is easy for him to increase his muscle mass. He believes he is genetically gifted in having a muscular, powerful body.

After finishing his weight training, he stretches for another ten minutes. This concludes his morning workout. He begins his second training session in the afternoon.

Afternoon Training Sessions

He begins with shadow kickboxing. He then kicks and punches various bags, and does a lot of sparring with his training partners. This is done for about two hours. The next day he trains in submission grappling techniques.

Ruas practices chokes, armbars, leg locks, neck cranks, ankle locks, takedowns, throws, and standup and ground grappling.

He also trains in various escapes and reversals. This training session takes two to three hours to complete. The following training session, he returns to kickboxing and related training. To sum it up: one day he trains in kickboxing, the next day in grappling.

He trains twice per day, training five to six hours a day when he is preparing for a fight.

This training routine is followed six days per week. He rests one day per week.

Ruas follows this routine for two months. Frequently he changes his exercises and training routines to avoid boredom and staleness.

Ruas trains for strength, speed, flexibility, and endurance. He considers endurance training one of the most significant and meaningful parts of his training, noting that he has seen many good fighters lose fights because they lack conditioning and stamina. "I will never lose a fight because I lack endurance and conditioning," he says.

Diet

Ruas eats a lot. His favorite foods are fruit, vegetables, egg whites, chicken, and fish—and, as all good Brazilians do, he eats lots of rice and beans. He avoids fried foods and sweets. Ruas drinks about five glasses of milk a day. He also drinks protein shakes. A typical breakfast for Marco is: fresh fruit, six egg whites, two pieces of whole wheat toast, and a large protein shake.

History

Ruas began training in *judo* at the age of thirteen. After studying *judo* for a few months, he turned to boxing. He then began studying *Tae Kwon Do* and various martial arts. One such martial art was *capoeira*, which was founded by Africans who lived in Brazil. He studied this martial art for five years and became very skillful in it.

Ruas also studied *Luta Livre*, a combination of freestyle wrestling, Greco-Roman wrestling, *judo*, and *jujitsu*. It is practiced without a jacket. In Brazil, there is a fierce rivalry between the *Luta Livre* grapplers and the followers of Gracie *jujitsu*.

Another martial art sport Ruas excels in is *Muay Thai* boxing. He prefers to kick and punch in a fight, but he is prepared to fight on the ground if he has to. He is a superb submission grappler.

At this time, Ruas is a *Vale Tudo* stylist. He is a three-time *Vale Tudo* super fight champion and his record is 14 victories and 1 draw. He was also the winner of the Ultimate Fighting Championship VII and four-time Brazilian *Muay Thai* champion.

His goal is to fight for four more years and to become the best fighter that he can be. Another goal is to open a gym and teach his Ruas *Vale Tudo* Fighting System.

Ruas is a devoted family man. He has a lovely wife and two beautiful daughters.

Marco Ruas is an outstanding fighter and I am certain that this magnificent fighting champion will accomplish all of his goals in the near future.

This material originally appeared in the June 1998 issue of Inside Karate.

PART 7

Weapons Training

New Training with Used Tires

Sean C. Ledig

To all you wannabe *arnistas*, *kendoka*, *kobudoka*, and other aspiring weapons students: if you like being a baton twirler, don't read this chapter.

To anyone who is serious about learning to use a weapon in combat, and doing more than showing off for a bunch of drunks by spinning a pair of *nunchaku* at a keg party: read on.

No one ever got to be proficient with a weapon without learning to make contact with something. Just swinging a stick, chain, or sword around and thinking that you'll magically know what to do if you ever really need to use it will probably get you hurt. If you're lucky, that's all that will happen to you.

Fortunately, there is a cheap and easy way to develop the contact skills you need. In fact, you can usually find the materials you need littering the highways and byways of America. Two words: used tires.

My first experience with tire training came four years ago, from my senior and teacher, John "*Sifu Gumbo*" Angeles. In addition to being my senior in lion's roar *kung fu*, Angeles also held a second *dan* in a classical style of *jujitsu*, and was familiar with many of the classical Japanese weapons. Having always wanted to learn to use a *katana*, or samurai sword, I offered to teach John a *tai chi gim* (sword) set I knew if he would teach me to use a *bokken*, or wooden practice sword.

John taught me the basic footwork and a few cuts, then left me with this recommendation: Take a tire and cut it in half. Then put it on a table about waist high and try cutting it with your *bokken*.

I followed his advice, and with a note of pride in his voice, John commented on the telltale black skid marks on my *bokken* the next time we got together. At home, I decided to experiment. I hung a tire from a post and practiced strikes with the double-ended staff, another weapon John taught me. Later, I started using the tire to practice with my *kali* sticks, as well as wooden knives and eventually, *nunchaku* and three-sectioned staff.

Tire *Makiwaras* and Dummies

Along with being cheap, tires are also versatile. Put a masonry wheel on a bench grinder or a power saw, and the tires can be cut into any number of usable shapes. They can be cut into halves or quarters and bolted onto a post or wall at about knee height to practice low kicks. Or the pieces can be put on a table and used to practice overhead strikes with a stick or *bokken*.

True, leg kicks and overhead strikes aren't flashy, but they are effective and will save your life if you get proficient. At a Dan Inosanto seminar held in Tampa, Florida, last year, guru Dan told those in attendance about an *arnista* of his acquaintance who practiced overhead strikes almost to the exclusion of every-

thing else. But he was so proficient in that one technique that he didn't need anything else. No one got close enough to try anything without getting clocked with an overhead blow.

If you're too lazy to be bothered with cutting up a tire, then you can simply tie or bolt it to the base of a *makiwara* and use it for kicking. Or, just hang it from a fence or post and start whacking away with your chosen weapon. A tire *makiwara* can be as intricate as you're willing to make it. I've seen some tires bolted together and strung up from a tree like a hanging man.

One of the most original designs I've seen is one that looks like a scarecrow, which I borrowed from my friend Dave Jones, a member of the Society for Creative Anachronism. Though derisively referred to as "the world's most heavily armed keg party" and "a fight choreographer's nightmare," I have to give them credit for their attempts to keep the ancient martial arts of Europe alive. Though I'm not a member, I have crossed swords with several of them and I can say some are very proficient with their chosen weapons. If the tire dummy I borrowed from Dave

The author demonstrates how the tire dummy can be used for practicing with a *bokken* (upper left), staff (upper middle), *kali* sticks (upper right), practice knife (lower left), and *nunchaku* (lower right).

is an indication of their training methods, I'm sure they can give many conventional Asian martial artists a run for their money.

Getting Started

Hitting a tire with any weapon should not be entered into hastily. The student should start out with only basic strikes with nonflexible weapons. Save the more complicated moves and combinations for later. It takes time to develop the strength necessary to hold onto a weapon when striking a tire. Remember the first time you hit a *makiwara* or heavy bag? Remember how it felt when you just started out and your wrist collapsed on contact? The same thing can happen here if you rush the training.

Also, striking a tire with a weapon is an excellent means of hand conditioning and should be approached with the same common sense and preparation. If you don't know any simple *chi kung*, I'd suggest you find a teacher so you can learn to focus on your hands. This will also prevent injury. Don't ask me how—I just know that when I am practicing *chi kung* regularly, my hands feel harder and my palms are stronger without doing any other exercises. You should also take the time to stretch your wrists and fingers before hitting the tire. If you don't know how, find a book or a teacher and learn some exercises. Finally, before you hit anything with a weapon, bare hand, or foot, get yourself a good brand of or recipe for *dit da jow* and learn to use it.

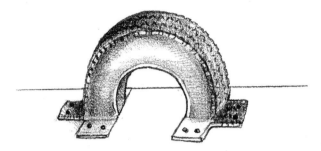

This sketch shows how a tire can be used as a leg conditioning device. Above, the tire is cut in half and bolted to a wall or post. It can also be placed on a table for practicing overhead cuts with a *bokken*.

Before I close, I have to admit there is one problem with tire training. You'll have less time to play around, twirling your *nunchaku* or staff like a high school drum majorette. But all I can say is, which is more important: learning to look good, or learning to use your weapon for its intended purpose, namely self-defense?

This material originally appeared in the April 1999 issue of Inside Kung-Fu.

PART 8

Injuries

Ancient Chinese Remedies for Today's Injuries

Linda J. Woodward

The connection between Oriental medicine and martial arts is centuries old and includes complete and effective systems of herbology, acupuncture, acupressure, massage, and bone setting. Each of these healing arts includes traumatology (treatment of injuries), treatment of disease, and methods for increasing longevity, energy, and stamina.

Herbology is further divided into internal and external applications. Injuries are often treated internally with teas, syrups, or pills and externally with poultices, liniments, and plasters at the same time. For stamina and longevity, prized herbs and roots are brewed into a variety of recipes, many of which have remained the valued secrets of families or martial systems for generations.

The most common injuries in martial arts are to muscle, ligaments, tendons, or bones. If the injury is treated immediately, thus preventing or relieving a major block in the energy and bloodflow, the complications can be lessened or even prevented.

For Bruising and Muscle Strain

Western medicine recommends icing a bruise. Eastern medicine recommends rubbing it. Bruising is internal bleeding that causes a congestion of damaged cells and blood. The injury will heal more rapidly if the stagnation is removed. An acupuncturist will often bleed or cup this type of injury to actually remove the damaged cells from the body.

Another method is to massage the injury with a liniment such as *dit da jow*. Always massage from the center of the injury outward and toward the heart. Sometimes you can watch the bruise disappear as you break up the congestion. *Jow* should be massaged into the area frequently and liberally until the bruise is gone. It should never be used on open wounds. Taken internally, it can be poisonous.

Dit da jow means "hit wine" because it is an injury medicine with an alcohol base. There are many brands of *jow* on the market. Many herbal suppliers will have their own formulas. Request their best quality. It may cost a little more, but it's worth the extra pennies to find the best brand. An excellent *jow* has amazing results on many injuries. Many martial arts masters and practitioners make their own formulas. The recipes are handed down from master to disciple and closely guarded.

Dit da jow is the liniment of choice for bruising, inflammation, swelling, and blood clotting. Applied to an injury immediately, it can actually prevent tissue damage.

Liniments for Ligament and Tendon Injury

Sprains, torn ligaments, and tendon injuries are common in grappling systems such as *chin na*, *jujitsu*, *judo*, and *aikido*. Often these injuries are more painful and take longer to heal than broken bones. The preferred liniment when dealing with tendons, ligaments, and even broken bones is Zeng Gu Shui. Zeng Gu Shui is a hot liniment that relaxes tendons and muscles and promotes the healing of traumatic injuries such as fractures, sprains, ligament tears, and deep bone bruising. It is also useful for the type of knee pain caused by overtraining or improper posture. Zeng Gu Shui is not massaged into the injury, but applied with a piece of cotton. It can be reapplied several times during the day.

Chronic injuries or severe sprains or ligament damage should be treated aggressively. First, wash and dry the wound. Then apply Zeng Gu Shui to a cotton pad or paper towel and place on the injured area. Cover the area with plastic wrap and leave it on

for ten to twenty minutes. You will feel heat within minutes. This application can be repeated twice in one day. Keep in mind that Zeng Gu Shui can be irritating to sensitive skin and can even cause burning if left in place for too long, especially using this method. You must check the treated area frequently until you learn what your body's tolerance is to the formula.

Liniments for Muscle Aches and Pains

Minor muscular aches and pains are relieved by oil-based liniments that can be rubbed onto or massaged into the muscles and left on for as long as necessary. Some come in a liquid form, and others in a salve. Most of these remedies feel warm as they increase circulation, relax tight muscles, and facilitate the removal of congestion and dead cells from the affected area.

When applying these remedies be careful to avoid open cuts and mucous membrane areas such as the eyes. Always wash your hands well with soap and warm water after applying. Inadvertently touching your eyes while a trace remains on your fingers can cause tearing and stinging.

Tiger Balm

Often referred to as "Chinese Vicks," Tiger Balm is good for minor soreness or muscle aches. Tiger Balm comes in three strengths, starting with the mildest, which is the white. Next in strength is red Tiger Balm. The strongest is called Imperial Balm. Tiger Balm comes in jars and in little tins that can be added to your personal first aid kit. It is easy to find and is often carried by health food stores and Chinese markets. Recently it has been appearing in Western drugstores as a remedy for arthritis.

Some athletes like to use Tiger Balm to warm up their muscles before training. If you do this, remember that the salve does have the distinctive odor of camphor. Also, it can make you very unpopular if you transfer it to an unsuspecting partner's hands during practice.

The excellent muscle liniments White Flower, Po Sum On Medicated Oil, and Kwan Loong Oil are stronger than Tiger Balm and are excellent for massaging sore muscles. These liquid liniments work well on large areas such as the back. Again, be careful that these oils do not come in contact with a mucous membrane. They can be applied as liberally and as frequently as desired.

Plasters

A variety of plasters on the market contain exceptional formulas and are unrivaled in their convenience of application. They usually come individually wrapped, six to twelve in a box. These cellophane-wrapped cloth patches covered with herbal ointment readily adhere to clean, dry skin. For small areas, such as finger injuries, they can be cut to size with scissors and wrapped around the injured joint.

Hua Tuo Anti Contusion and Rheumatism Plaster is a relatively mild plaster for muscular aches and rheumatic pains. It works well for stiff neck and shoulders and can be left on for up to twenty-four hours.

Musk and Tiger Bone Plaster (She Xiang Zhui Feng Gao) is a stronger plaster, and is good for swelling and bruises. It can be left on for up to twenty-four hours.

Plaster for Bruise and Analgesic (Die Da Zhi Tong Gao, or "Traumatic Injury Stop Plaster") is for acute bruises, sprains, fractures, and traumatic swelling. It also is good for muscle strain and neuralgia.

Kou Pi Plaster (Go Pi Gao, or "Dog Skin Plaster") works well for severe sprains, strains, and contusions. The herbs in this plaster are suspended in a gummy base. Heat the plaster in a steamer or a very low oven until the herbs become sticky. Then open the plaster and press the gummy side onto the injured area. Be careful not to burn the skin. This plaster can be left in place for ten to twenty minutes. It is very messy and can stain clothing.

Magic Plaster (Shen Xian Jin Bu Huan Gao, or "Miraculous Spirit Not to Be Exchanged for Gold") is an excellent pain reliever. It is good for contusions, muscle strain or sprain, aching joints, numbness, and weakness of muscles. It is a cloth with resin in the center. You need to steam the cloth until the resin melts and then spread the mixture across the fabric. After checking the temperature, apply the plaster to the affected area. It can be resteamed and used a second time.

Remedies for Bleeding

Traditional Chinese medicine provides two popular remedies to stop bleeding and speed coagulation. Yunnan Paiyao is the best known. It comes as a powder that can be sprinkled directly onto the wound after it has been cleaned and disinfected.

Yunnan Paiyao is also taken internally with alcohol to break up the stagnation of blood and energy in the case of bruises or sprains. The tiny pink pill found in each bottle is used only in the case of life-threatening trauma such as bleeding from a gunshot wound. The primary ingredient in Yunnan Paiyao is tenchi ginseng or pseudo ginseng.

Tenchi ginseng can be purchased both in a raw form and in a steamed form. The steamed tenchi is a blood tonic, and is not useful for first aid. Raw tenchi can be sprinkled on a wound to stop bleeding. Raw tenchi is actually the main ingredient in most internal "hit medicines," and can be used internally to help dissolve stagnation of blood and *chi* identified by bruising and swelling. It should always be included in a first aid kit.

Herbal remedies can be as powerful as chemical medicines. If you have serious medical conditions, especially circulatory problems such as high blood pressure or heart disease, or if you are pregnant, use herbal remedies with the approval or under the supervision of your doctor or acupuncturist.

Pregnant women should not use *dit da jow*, Zeng Gu Shui, or any of the plasters. Self-treatment is not recommended as a substitute for professional medical help in the case of serious injury; however, it can be a good support system for conventional Western treatment. Certainly, the use of plasters and liniments for the relief of pain is much healthier than the use of pharmaceutical drugs.

All Oriental philosophies stress the importance of balance. The yin and the yang must exist in harmony with each other. Fighting skills are the yang energy. The development of healing skills will provide balancing yin energy to your personal training. Strive always for harmony.

This material originally appeared in the May 1998 issue of Inside Kung-Fu.

Coming Back from Ankle Injuries

David S. Bader, M.D.

An ankle injury to the martial artist is potentially devastating. The lower extremities are an integral source of speed and power for both offensive and defensive maneuvers. On average, one out of every ten patients seen in the emergency department has sports-related trauma.

Ankle trauma is the number-one injury associated with sports today. There are over ten million ankle sprains annually in the United States. Depending on the type of injury, treatment is generally straightforward and surgery is seldom required. Joint instability, however, is a major complication, especially in the athletic patient.

This chapter offers a brief overview of the causes, complications, and management of the acute ankle sprain. It is not a comprehensive review of ankle injuries and should not be regarded as a substitute for evaluation and recommendations of your physician.

Mechanism of Injury

The ankle is constructed like a door hinge, leaving it vulnerable to twisting injuries referred to as *inversion* or *eversion* injury. Inversion, or internal rotation, is the most common injury seen, accounting for approximately 85 percent of all ankle trauma. The injury most commonly occurs as the heel strikes the ground and the foot turns inward, straining the anterior talofibular ligament.

Common maneuvers predisposing an athlete to this type of injury are jumping and flying kicks, turning attacks, and running. The severity of the sprain depends on the amount of twisting and the number of ligaments involved.

The second most common ankle injury is an eversion, which results in the disruption of several ligaments, including the anterolateral and calcaneofibular ligaments. This most commonly occurs during sweeping, trapping, and instep kicks, as the toes become trapped and the ankle is pulled up and forward.

Management

Treatment is composed of several steps that are initiated prior to seeing your doctor. Immediate measures include Rest, Ice, Compression, and Elevation (RICE), the aim of which is to minimize bleeding and swelling.

• **Rest**—This is a difficult concept for most martial artists, but a necessary one to speed recovery and to maintain joint stability. Following evaluation by a medical doctor, the athlete with a mild to moderate sprain should bear weight on the affected ankle when pain permits to avoid a tight heel cord that limits ankle motion. The athlete with a third-degree sprain must not allow the ankle to bear any weight and should be seen by an orthopedic surgeon.

• **Ice**—Immediate application of ice following the injury is essential and is most effective if applied intermittently. The general approach is application of ice for a minimum of thirty minutes every four to six hours for the next forty-eight to seventy-two hours after the injury. Cooling device options include ice packs, whirlpool ice water, iced wet towels, and commercially available cold packs. Chipped ice performs consistently and cools the most efficiently. Moist heat can be applied after the first seventy-two hours until inflammation subsides.

• **Compression**—Wrap the ankle in an elastic bandage, being careful not to apply too much pressure, which may cause a tourniquet effect and limit bloodflow to the extremity. Compression should be removed during ice treatments to allow for optimal penetration of the ice. The compression wrap doesn't need the ice: the injured ankle does.

• **Elevation**—The ankle must be raised above the level of the heart to allow for unimpeded bloodflow back to the heart, thereby reducing swelling. Propping the foot on your gym bag is not enough. This must be continued for three to five days after the injury for all but first-degree sprains.

In addition to applying RICE measures, you may use pain (analgesic) and anti-inflammatory medicines when injured. Once the acute swelling subsides, an airsplint brace or taping can be used to improve stability. These mechanical supports can be continued for one to two weeks. The more extensive the injury, the longer the recovery time. It should be noted that airsplints, taping, or casting should not be applied until after the acute swelling subsides.

Grade III injuries (and some Grade II injuries) may require casting for one to two weeks, after which time rehabilitation is started. Approximately 25 percent of Grade III injuries have recurrent ankle instability and may benefit from reconstructive surgery. Surgery as a routine, however, is generally not indicated to repair acute ankle injuries. Yet, it may be appropriate for the active martial artist with recurrent injuries or those who wish correction to avoid recurrence. Consult your doctor.

Ankle sprains are often regarded as trivial by martial artists. Several reviews indicate that as much as 70 percent of athletes have recurrent ankle sprains and that over 50 percent have significant disability that leads to impairment of their athletic performance. It is for these very reasons that a proper approach toward injury prevention and rehabilitation is required.

Rehabilitation focuses on restoring normal motion, strength, and balance. Early intervention expedites return to sports and work and does not compromise stability of the ankle joint. The exercises are designed to develop coordination of the calf muscles and to overcome any sensory nerve defects from the injury.

A focus of treatment is to avoid delays in weight bearing on the injured ankle. Early weight bearing has been shown to decrease cord tightening, ankle edema, and muscle atrophy. While early range-of-motion activity is beneficial, unreasonable activity can extend the injury. These exercises and the extent of activity that can reasonably be tolerated should be discussed with your doctor and physical therapist.

Complications

As noted earlier, chronic ankle instability can be present in up to 25 percent of patients sustaining acute ankle injuries. This has been shown to cause degenerative arthritis of the ankle in 80 percent of cases.

Prevention

Following the specific recommendations of your physician, support with custom orthotics may reduce the frequency of recurrent ankle sprains. A heel wedge, elastic anklet, or ankle taping with high-top shoes or a combination of low-top shoes and laced ankle stabilizers may be recommended during activity for athletes with recurrent inversion injuries. Ankle wrapping starts with the bandage at the base of the toes and extends to midway up the calf.

The ankle should be free to move in flexion and extension (up and down) but limited in regard to inversion or eversion (side to side).

Exercises

The following exercises can be done within one or two days of most injuries and continued for four to six weeks. Your doctor can advise you when it is safe to begin.

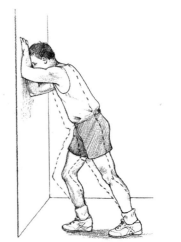

To stretch the heel cord, stand at arm's length from a wall with your hands resting against the wall at shoulder height. Extend the injured foot behind you. Point the toes straight ahead with the feet flat on the ground and straighten your rear knee. Bend the arms at the elbow and flex forward by bending the forward knee. Hold for twenty seconds. Repeat with opposite leg. Do this up to three to four times a day.

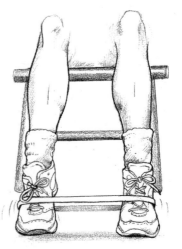

Sit in a chair or on a stool so your feet clear the floor. Place a stretched bungee cord or rubber band around both feet. Move both feet outward simultaneously so you can feel the resistance against the cord. Return. Repeat twenty-five times, up to three to four times a day.

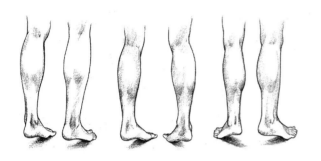

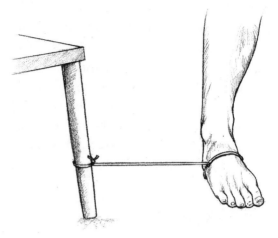

Calf raises: stand on the floor with your toes straight ahead and slowly rise on your tiptoes. Repeat this with your toes pointed inward, then outward. Repeat each position twenty-five times, up to three times a day.

Tie one end of a piece of rubber tubing around a piece of furniture. Tie the other end around the injured foot. In a seated position, pull the tubing toward you as far as it will go. Repeat in the opposite direction. Repeat each direction fifteen to twenty times, up to three times a day.

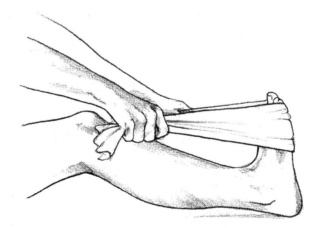

Sit with your legs straight in front of you. Loop a towel around the ball of one foot, holding the ends in each hand. Without bending the knee, give a continuous pull on the towel for ten seconds, gently stretching the calf and ankle. Relax. Repeat on the other foot. Repeat each side twenty times, up to three times a day.

Conclusion

The study of the martial arts is a lifelong commitment. The health and well-being of body, mind, and spirit are integral to that commitment. The ability to avoid or at least treat potentially devastating injuries is part of that commitment to overall health and fitness.

This material originally appeared in the August 1998 issue of Inside Kung-Fu.

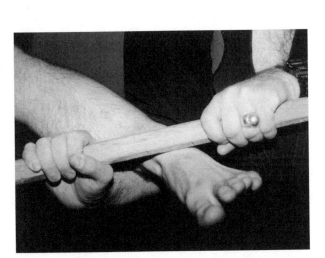

Robert Platukis demonstrates a short stick trap.

Thomas Costello shows destructive potential in this execution of a front kick.

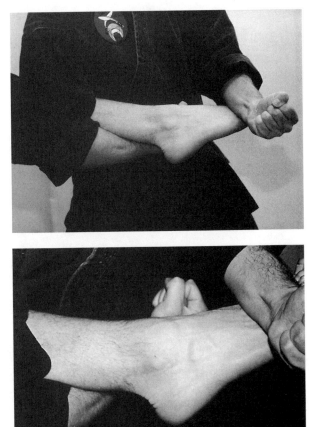

The tension and strain on the ankle is evident here as the author demonstrates an ankle trap.

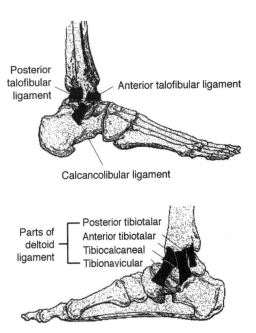

Exercising During Illness

Joseph J. Estwanik, M.D., and William A. Primos, M.D.

It is well known that exercise can improve health, but even elite athletes are grounded by sicknesses like the flu, measles, and colds. Usually, people do not feel like exercising during an illness.

Many athletes, however, especially those who are competitively motivated, have reasons to continue training or competing while sick. Some feel they will get out of shape if they skip a few days in the gym. Others may have an upcoming game or competition they don't want to miss. So just what is the best avenue to follow during an illness? Should you rest, or is it OK to exercise? Can it be dangerous to exercise with an illness? Are there specific types of diseases that are especially hazardous for exercisers?

Research studies have shown that exercise worsens respiratory illnesses like the common cold, bronchitis, and pneumonia. Intense exercise during such a sickness can cause increased cough, wheezing, and shortness of breath. People who have illnesses with

fever, vomiting, and/or diarrhea may get dehydrated during their illness. Intense exercise causes additional loss of fluid through sweating. Heat builds up because the body can't cool itself properly. This can set the stage for heatstroke, which can be lethal. Due to the risk of heatstroke, intense exercise should be avoided by anyone with an illness that consists of diarrhea, vomiting, or fever. If you are running a fever, it is not wise to work out. Rest; use acetaminophen, ibuprofen, or aspirin; and drink fluids to maximize your recovery.

Children should not ingest aspirin during febrile illnesses to avoid the possibility of contracting Reye's syndrome. Viral illnesses with the classic symptoms of sore throat, runny nose, and sinus congestion are not improved by antibiotics. Should unusual manifestations appear, schedule a visit with your doctor.

Sometimes a virus called *coxsackievirus* can cause an illness that mimics the flu. This virus may infect the heart muscles and cause myocarditis. If people with this heart infection participate in strenuous activities, they may suffer heart failure or a heart attack, which can kill them. Due to this possible complication, individuals suffering flu-like illnesses with fever and muscle aches should avoid strenuous exercise until they feel well.

Another widespread disease that may have a severe complication is infectious mononucleosis, or "mono." Fatigue, prolonged sore throat, and swollen lymph nodes could signal a case of mono. An enlarged spleen, which often accompanies this illness, is a definite signal to avoid contact activities, as a ruptured spleen causes potentially fatal internal bleeding. A swollen, spongy spleen may rupture or "pop" during strenuous athletics, especially contact sports, where the abdomen may be hit forcefully. Therefore, athletes should avoid strenuous and contact sports for at least one month after coming down with mono, assuming the spleen is not found by their examining doctor to be enlarged. A common blood test can easily screen for mono infections.

A good general guideline for determining whether it is safe to participate in physical activities during your illness is the "neck check." If all of your symptoms are above the neck, like a runny nose, scratchy throat, or an earache, then exercise is probably safe. Start exercising at low intensity for several minutes. If you do not begin to feel worse, then increase the exertion level.

However, if symptoms are located below the neck, such as muscle aches, fever, chills, weakness, diarrhea, or a deep cough, avoid exercise. Otherwise, you risk worsening your illness and causing severe complications. Rest will also speed recovery as you give your body a chance to heal itself rather than diverting energy to exercise.

You should also consider whether your illness may infect other participants on your team or in the gym. Some illnesses can be easily transferred to others through invisible respiratory droplets. Measles and common colds are such diseases. These viruses can be transmitted through the air when the infected person coughs or sneezes near someone else. People with measles should not be around others for four days after the rash first appears.

Illnesses are sometimes unknowingly spread to others by seemingly innocent means, such as shared ice buckets, drinking containers, and towels. Infections can be effectively decreased by the use of disposable cups, individual water bottles, and towels.

This material was adapted from Dr. Joseph J. Estwanik and Dr. William A. Primos's book Sports Medicine for the Combat Arts.

PART 9

Sparring

To Spar or Not to Spar

Is That the Question?

Sang H. Kim

One of the most controversial debates in martial arts is the place full-contact sport sparring has in martial arts training. Many traditional and self-defense oriented teachers would have you believe that sparring is a useless part of martial arts training. In this chapter, I will explain ten basic reasons why full-contact sparring is essential to learning how to react efficiently in a real confrontation.

The Ability to Perform Under Pressure

By practicing continuous (without stopping for points scored) full-contact sparring, you learn how to deal with the unrelenting attacks of an opponent. For the length of the match, you have to create an effective offense according to your opponent's fighting style. At the same time, you must respond to the opponent's attacks by defending yourself accurately and forcefully—or risk getting injured by a full-contact strike. Although participants wear protective gear, a full-contact kick to the head will absolutely result in a knockout.

The Ability to Adapt Quickly to Your Opponent's Actions

Because free sparring is not prearranged (like self-defense practice), your opponent can use any type of permitted attack. You must be prepared to counter an endless variety of movements, adapting to your opponent's style and timing. Although a street fighter has fewer rules limitations, an experienced sparring competitor can respond more quickly and calmly to unknown situations through full-contact practice.

The Ability to Protect Yourself When Injured

In almost every sparring match, as in almost every self-defense situation, you will get hit and possibly hurt. Whether it is a bruised foot, banged shin, bump on the head, black eye, or something more serious, you have to know how to continue in spite of the pain. Competition teaches you this principle. Watch sport competitors leave the arena after a sparring competition—most will be sporting some sort of bandage or ice pack. Injuries, and the pain associated with them, cause the human body to instinctively shut down. If you are not prepared for the mental and physical shock of an injury, you might be unprepared to defend yourself when hurt. Of course, this does not mean you should spar with a serious injury; but it does mean you should learn to not get distracted by physical contact.

The Ability to Withstand an Opponent's Blows and Respond Calmly

Novice students often imagine themselves stepping onto the mat and taking on an opponent with the serene calm of the black belts they have watched spar. Once they face their first opponent, reality sets in. When you get hit, your natural response is not calmness, but rather anger—a quick instinctive flash that urges you to exact revenge on your attacker, even if it is your classmate. Learning to overcome this flash of anger is essential to both competing and defending yourself successfully. With experience, you can take your opponent's blows in stride and counterattack calmly and correctly without emotions.

The Ability to Think Clearly Under Duress

In other words, don't panic. The first time you face someone who wants to hurt you, even in a competitive match, you may suddenly forget everything you ever learned and resort to hopelessly fending off an ever-increasing rain of blows. Or perhaps you may find yourself tied in knots, thinking of what you should have done instead of actually executing your strategy. To overcome the instinctive fear you feel when confronted with a physical threat, you must face this fear and practice controlling it in a secure environment. There is probably no better environment for this than competitive sparring. Your skills are meaningless if you can't use them in a stressful situation.

Mental and Physical Endurance

Regular sparring builds physical and emotional endurance. Physical endurance is important in confrontations when your opponent is larger than you or a more experienced fighter. Through sparring with a variety of partners, you also learn to pace yourself and outlast tough opponents. Mental endurance is necessary in order to concentrate fully on your opponent's actions and to read his intentions, as well as to formulate your own strategy when the odds are against you.

The Ability to Strike with Power and Accuracy

Hitting the heavy bag is useful but, as the saying goes, heavy bags don't hit back. Nor do they move around and try to avoid your attacks. If you want to learn to apply your skills realistically, you must apply them against a live opponent, just as you would in a real situation. Of course, applying deadly skills (like eye gouges and throat strikes) to your partner is impossible, but sparring does give you a forum to apply a limited number of skills against active resistance from your opponent. You quickly learn what works and what doesn't when the pressure is on in the ring.

The Ability to Move Quickly

Practicing your skills in training drills improves your form, but only the pressure of a realistic confrontation can create the speed you need to attack and defend successfully. When your opponent launches an attack, you must be quick in both your reaction (to defend yourself) and also your action (to counter your opponent's attack). Through sparring, you develop speed and timing in evasion, defense, strategy, footwork, and counterattacking.

The Ability to Spot Vulnerabilities and Exploit Them

Through sparring, you learn to spot weaknesses in your opponent's defense, to read his next move, to detect bad habits, and to intercept telegraphed movements. These are intangible skills that you can learn only from experience. They are essential to defeating bigger, stronger assailants such as the one you may meet in a street confrontation.

The Ability to Apply Your Knowledge

When you are proficient at sparring, you can easily apply your skills, speed, timing, and strategy to any situation, whether competitive or confrontational. To enhance your self-defense skills, you can modify your sparring practice to include techniques that may not be legal in your style. Some techniques, while not legal in sport competition, can be safely applied in full-contact sparring.

Conclusion

Full-contact sparring is certainly no substitute for practical self-defense skills, but it can absolutely enhance your ability to defend yourself. By giving you a chance to put yourself at physical risk, full-contact sparring creates a realistic threat and gives you the opportunity and the tools to learn to control that threat and also your responses to it. In this sense, self-defense and full-contact sparring are one in intent and spirit.

This material originally appeared in the April 1999 issue of Martial Arts Illustrated.